Tree Form, Size and Colour

*A guide to
selection,
planting
and
design*

Other titles from E & FN Spon

Amenity Landscape Management
A resources handbook
Ralph Cobham

Beazley's Design & Detail of the Space Between Buildings
A. Pinder and A. Pinder

Caring for our Built Heritage
Conservation in practice: a review of conservation schemes carried out by County Councils in England and Wales in association with District Councils
Edited by T. Haskell

Le Corbusier
An analysis of form
G. Baker

Crime Prevention through Housing Design
Edited by P. Stollard

Countryside Conservation
2nd Edition
Bryn Green

Countryside Management
Peter Bromley

Countryside Recreation
A handbook for managers
Peter Bromley

Elements of Visual Design in the Landscape
S. Bell

Emerging Concepts in Urban Space Design
G. Broadbent

Environmental Planning for Site Development
Anne Beer

Frank Lloyd Wright and Japan
The role of Japan in the shaping of Frank Lloyd Wright's organic architecture
K. Nute

Fungal Diseases of Amenity Turf Grasses
3rd Edition
J. Drew Smith, N. Jackson and A. Woolhouse

The Garden City
Past, present and future
S. Ward

The Golf Course
Planning, design, construction and management
F. Hawtree

A Handbook of Segmental Paving
A. Lilley

Parking
A handbook of environmental design
J. McCluskey

The Green Book – Plant and Landscape Materials Price Guide
Building Materials Market Research

Spon's Landscape Contract Handbook
A guide to good practice and procedures in the management of lump-sum landscape contracts
H. Clamp

Spon's Landscape Handbook
Derek Lovejoy and Partners

Understanding Architecture through Drawing
B. Edwards

For more information on these and other titles please contact:
The Promotion Department, E. & F. N. Spon, 2–6 Boundary Row, London SE1 8HN.
Telephone 071–865–0066.

Tree Form, Size and Colour

*A guide to
selection,
planting
and
design*

BODFAN GRUFFYDD

E & FN SPON
An Imprint of Chapman & Hall

London · Glasgow · Weinheim · New York · Tokyo · Melbourne · Madras

**Published by E & FN Spon, an imprint of Chapman & Hall,
2-6 Boundary Row, London SE1 8HN, UK**

Chapman & Hall, 2-6 Boundary Row, London SE1 8HN, UK

Blackie Academic & Professional, Wester Cleddens Road, Bishopbriggs,
Glasgow G64 2NZ, UK

Chapman & Hall GmbH, Pappelallee 3, 69469 Weinheim, Germany

Chapman & Hall Inc., One Penn Plaza, 41st Floor, New York, NY10119, USA

Chapman & Hall Japan, Thomson Publishing Japan, Hirakawacho Nemoto
Building, 6F, 1-7-11 Hirakawa-cho, Chiyoda-ku, Tokyo 102, Japan

Chapman & Hall Australia, Thomas Nelson Australia, 102 Dodds Street, South
Melbourne, Victoria 3205, Australia

Chapman & Hall India, R. Seshadri, 32 Second Main Road, CIT East, Madras
600 035, India

First edition 1987
Paperback edition 1994

© 1987, 1994 J.St Bodfan Gruffydd

Printed in Great Britain at the University Press, Cambridge

ISBN 0 419 19610 2

A Catalogue record for this book is available from the British Library

Library of Congress Cataloging-in-Publication Data available

To the inspiration of Colwyn Faulkes

Contents

Foreword

I value the opportunity that my friend Bodfan Gruffydd has given me to contribute a preface to this particular work which is a distillation of his wide experience over more than forty years in the realm of trees and their place in all types of landscape and townscape. The author was involved in a wide range of projects during his appointment as landscape architect at the new towns of Harlow and Crawley before accepting a two year Harvard Fellowship at Dumbarton Oaks. Thence in private practice he was engaged in schemes embracing an extensive range of landscape problems such as requirements of hospitals, large and small gardens, country and urban parks, town and out of town shopping centres, various institutions and concerns including a development plan for an oil refinery on Southampton Water.

Clearly the question of amenity has been paramount in his work and his research sponsored by the Leverhulme Trust on the protection of historic landscapes has been specially noteworthy in implementing government policy.

I can also vouch for his forceful advocacy as a member of the Department of Transport Landscape Advisory Committee for Motorways and Trunk Roads of which I was Chairman, especially on matters affecting sensitive areas. On this Committee he represents the Landscape Institute of which he is a Past-president.

This manual, giving vital statistics of the trees suitable for chosen environments, will receive a ready welcome and become a respected reference source for those who seek to know the best trees to plant in particular sites with the prospect that they will thrive.

Sir George Taylor, DSc, FRS, VMH
Formerly Director of the Royal Botanic Gardens at Kew

Preface

This is a book about trees: trees as a major element in the art of designing gardens and the great outdoors; the beauty of trees in foliage, flower and fruit; their form and size; their scale and consequent ability to enrich the localities in which they grow. It deals with the individual characteristics of trees, both visual and physiological, and their demands and tolerances as elements in the design of landscape.

Designed landscape is a living art form, constantly changing. It is only through understanding the nature of its constituant materials and the way in which they develop over the years, that the designer is likely to realize his ultimate ideas in maturity; only by understanding the behaviour of the organic forces is it possible to plan subsequent management satisfactorily.

Together with landform and water, trees are the most important element in the landscape of temperate climates, having a reassuring stability and historical life. I started looking critically at them early in my career as a landscape designer. I found a number of good books on trees but nowhere did I find a single volume giving all the essential information for the use of trees as a designer's tool, readily available, in simple reference form. So I started to catalogue the various facts about trees which I found I needed to know in my work.

I wanted to know about the size and shape of individual trees and their siting: whether useful for shelter, as background planting and especially as elements in the furnishing of a garden; their main interest and season of special excellence; their density and texture of foliage; growth rate; soil preference, in shade or sun; air/soil tolerances and any unusual characteristics.

From the considerable collections of trees that I looked at I selected some 300 species and varieties. These include native and exotic trees of various forms – broad and narrow spreading, conical, spire shaped, columnar, weeping – helpful in the composition of landscape designs. Native trees are important in the conservation of wildlife; exotic forms were brought in to fill gaps. Then I took many photographs to identify the various shapes and foliage patterns.

Acknowledgements

I would like to express my gratitude to the many friends and colleagues who have helped me in various ways, over the years, to achieve this work. The late Oliver Slocock showed me his special collection of treasured columnar trees; Charles Coe was most helpful with advice on more difficult trees which nurserymen may be unlikely to grow; Robert Holden took many of the better photographs and his lovely wife helped in indexing them; Rosemary Angel provided helpful references and details; Jeremy Purseglove went through the tables with a tooth comb, which helped no end with ecology and naming; June Hebden arranged the index and Edward Piper gave early advice on the format; John White was inspirational in suggesting the USM formula for determining planting distances, and he, Malcolm Scott, and Charles Erskine have been most helpful with identification, while David Hunt has so kindly and exhaustively checked the nomenclature. Finally, but for Sir George Taylor's encouragement I doubt if the book would ever have got off the ground. In consequence readers will appreciate that any mistakes they spot are mine!

Introduction

THE DESIGN REQUIREMENT

The landscape designer's first aim is to create a landscape framework of a semi-permanent and renewable nature within which provision may be made for a variety of activities: grazing animals (as in parkland); recreation of all kinds, terrestial or aquatic; the conservation of threatened ecosystems; farming; gardening and indeed for healthy urban life. For this the existing topography may be considered satisfactory or the landform may need to be moulded to pleasing contours and hollowed out to form areas of water. Then the trees (or buildings) will be disposed to provide vertical scale and intimacy, in the enclosure of visually defined spaces – microlandscapes of varied and unique character appropriate to the different functions required of the design.

In this context trees assume immeasurable importance. Unlike buildings, trees take a generation 'to show themselves'. It is therefore of the greatest importance for the designer fully to comprehend their behaviour and mature state, bearing in mind that trees may be the only element available for the expression of this particular need.

So I am considering trees primarily as visual elements in landscape design – what they look like three dimensionally; how they bulk and mass and how they contribute to mood and the *genius loci*. In this, general appearance is more influential than detail for the author has always found it more helpful to be able to recognize a tree at a distance than by the minutiae of botanical description.

In composing the landscape picture height and shape come first, then colour, mass (transparency) and surface foliage character. These are designers' choices. But because of the organic nature of the element (trees) selection is limited within a number of environmental constraints e.g. soil structure, aspect and air and soil tolerance, which may require some compromise in the final choice.

This order of priorities has determined the format of reference adopted in the tables, which form the main part of the book. It will I hope be a useful reference for anyone, whether amateur or professional, who is considering the planting of a tree, whether it be in a small garden, a space in a town, along the roadside or as an element in any landscape design; it will serve as a guide to correct choice so that a beautiful tree may grow up healthily, without ever needing pruning! In this respect form (shape) and extent of spread is of paramount importance, for it is no good planting a tree which will develop a wide spread in a confined space, or along a road where its branches would interfere with buildings or the movement of traffic. Inevitably such a choice leads to pruning, lopping or other unsightly mutilation, prejudicial to the health of the tree as well as to recurring difficulties and expense in future maintenance management. Mutilation of this kind should not be confused with such traditional practices as rotational coppicing and pollarding, which can actually *prolong* the life of a tree.

DEFINITION

A tree has a trunk to support its branch system with a considerable head of foliage. When in leaf however, the trunk may not be seen if the tree is growing with plenty of space around it and provided the lower branches have not been removed by man or grazing animals. On the other hand, trees growing in groups or in woodland lose their lower branches as a result of competition, as each tree grows towards the light and, with its neighbours, casts too much shade for further growth of the lower branches which ultimately fall off.

MATURITY

A tree needs time and space to display its full beauty and magnificence. A young tree often develops a completely different character as it grows towards maturity. Maturity in this sense does not mean the age at which a tree first blossoms and sets seed, but rather the age when it develops its full character of branch structure and clothing of foliage. This mature stage can last for a considerable period, even hundreds of years when a tree enjoys its ecologically suitable environment, before gradually dying back to become stag-headed.

The age at which trees begin to assume this character of maturity is influenced by all the factors affecting growth. In adverse conditions a tree may well look mature before its time whereas favourable growth conditions may extend its adolescence. In average conditions trees begin to assume a mature character when they are half grown, that is when they reach half their ultimate height, apparently unaffected by rate of growth. One may expect to discern signs of maturity in large trees as they approach forty years of age, and in small trees at the earlier age of twenty years, give or take a few years either way.

The real beauty of a tree can only be seen in maturity, which it is impossible to hasten. In time this represents the life span of a healthy man or woman and should give pause for thought in any decision concerning the removal of a tree, affecting, as it would, not only those of our own generation but the progeny of two following generations as well.

As the components of our individual bodies, our hands, feet and faces, combine in a unique person so the roots and branches, twigs and leaves, flowers and fruits compose an individual tree. Amputation is equally damaging to the beauty of either, which brings me directly to one of the chief reasons for this book.

For too long we have seen trees mutilated in our streets and civic spaces, mercilessly lopped or repeatedly pollarded year after year, usually because the tree grows too big for its place. We come across trees planted in back gardens with the best intentions in the world, growing to shade and perhaps to drip honeydew over three neighbouring plots, ultimately creating a problem beyond the reasonable means of the trees' owner to solve. We see trees in small front gardens reduced to hat-stands without the faintest hope of ever again attaining their final glory. And this butchery still goes on – senselessly for it is unnecessary. We also see trees struggling for existence in situations foreign to their natural needs – poor, forlorn specimens, out of their element and doomed to slow death. Few things out of doors are more pathetic to look at than unhealthy trees.

It is not as if there were no choice in the matter. Today there is an immense variety of trees, deciduous and evergreen, of all shapes and sizes, of differing colour, leaf texture and seasonal interest from which to select a tree of the desired shape, to grow to the required size, in the soil available, to provide the amount of shade and the colour interest desired at a particular time of year.

TREE CHARACTER

Trees may be broad leaved or coniferous, deciduous or evergreen and have characteristic colour and shape.

Size

Here trees are separated into (1) *large trees* which normally grow taller than 50 ft (15 m) and (2) *small trees* which do not normally reach this height. Details of the height of individual trees are readily available in books mentioned in the Bibliography. The actual height a tree will ultimately reach, however, depends on all the factors affecting growth, as explained in the paragraph concerning maturity.

Form

Concern here is with the shape and form a tree acquires naturally, without pruning or training. There are broad spreading trees that grow wider than high and narrow spreading ones that grow higher than wide. There are conical shaped trees, spired and columnar trees, ovoid shaped trees and trees that weep.

Underground, root spread and behaviour

By and large root systems reflect those of the branches above. Developed root systems anchor trees in the ground and spread to collect moisture with dissolved plant foods. Anchor roots, especially tap roots, penetrate deeply, neither should be cut in the interests of the tree's stability. Feeding roots normally spread just beyond the outer extent of the branches above, where they are most active, 25% being in the top 150 mm of soil. The roots of greedy trees like ash or poplar may forage much further afield. Coniferous trees on the other hand, have more compact and fibrous root systems and do not normally forage far afield in search of food. Trees growing on clay, and especially if they require large quantities of water for their growth, can endanger the safety of buildings. In such circumstances, therefore, it is wise to consult the bibliography or take expert advice, before deciding on siting and species. Generally the radius of root spread may be taken as half USM (see p. 8).

Deciduous and evergreen trees

In these tables deciduous and evergreen trees are grouped together in the categories of size, their form being distinguished by appropriate symbols.

Colour

Individual trees have unique colour. Each has a main foliage colour and most have additional distinctive colour, displayed in bark, bud, unfolding and dying leaf, flower and fruit. The more flamboyant ones can be startling and indeed vulgar if indiscriminately mixed.

   Response to colour varies between individuals and according to prevailing light. Foliage colour of identical trees varies according to the stage of growth, soil moisture and pH (acidity/alkalinity), etc. Trees are grouped in general colour categories and to this extent the placing is subjective. Generally it will be found to be sufficient, according to the nature of the exercise. The colour illustrations attempt to indicate typical examples of foliage colour.

SITING AND DISPLAY

Here the physical, climatic and aesthetic functions of individual species are considered. Some trees provide useful shelter, others pleasing or useful backgrounds while many have unique individual excellence. Some share all three qualities. The beauty of some individual trees is lost when they are placed in close juxtaposition; such trees look well when sited as specimens within a framework of shelter or background planting, as pieces of furniture may be arranged in a gallery so that they can display their full complement of beauty.

DENSITY

There are trees with dense foliage and others which disclose their framework of supporting branches, while still others act as foils by no more than adding intricacy to views seen through their crowns.

Trees with dense foliage cast deep shade and obstruct views as well as suppressing plant life beneath. They are useful for framing views. Trees with open crowns on the other hand cast the least shade and views may be discerned through the canopy. Trees with loose foliage are intermediate.

Young trees have not had time to develop crowns characteristic of their species. As growth proceeds denser crowns develop; but these thin towards maturity when each species develops its characteristic beauty, which persists for the greater part of its life. This is the stage at which trees have been assessed in these tables. Foliage is least dense in youth and old age.

In Britain generally sunshine is sought rather than shade and so evergreen trees and trees with dense foliage are better sited away from buildings, especially if they are on the southern side. Where some cooling shade in summer is sought however, the best trees to choose are those of narrow spread and loose foliage. Trees with open texture provide delicate foils to buildings and enliven their ambience with dappled shade.

As would be expected leaf fall depends on the abundance and consequent denseness of leaves in the crown of the tree; the denser the crown the heavier the leaf fall. While accumulation of leaves on the ground varies with the size of the leaf; the larger the leaf the more they accumulate. See 'Growth' column in tables and illustrations.

LIGHT REFLECTION

Some trees glitter with light reflected from their shining leaves. Others appear dappled because their leaves' under surfaces are of contrasting colour or light reflection and turn in the breeze to reveal the alternating surfaces, giving the tree a lively character. There are trees with matt leaves which in extreme cases make the foliage look dull and uninteresting.

SURFACE PATTERN

Then there is the surface pattern of the tree's foliage. How is this to be described? As bristly, curly, clotted, crinkly, fluffy, feathery, ferny, faceted, woolly or how many other descriptions? A close-up photograph can be taken of the leaves but even this does not convey the impression of the tree from a distance because the photograph is still and the foliage is usually stirred by a breeze. Detailed photographs of trees' foliage are reproduced here but they should be taken as a guide to the description in the tables, they show what the surface pattern of the tree described looks like close to. They should not be misread. Concern is with the appearance of the tree in the distance, as part of an artistic composition and this is how they have been looked at and described.

GROWTH RATE

Interest now centres on the trees' rate of growth, for although planting may be for the generation after next – the grandchildrens' in fact – it is only human to be interested in what may be seen of a proper tree during the planter's lifetime.

Growth rate depends very much on soil, shelter, moisture, temperature and also on the care taken in site preparation, planting and subsequent maintenance. The rate of growth also varies during the life of the tree, being more rapid in early life, before slowing down as maturity is reached. As a guide to the rapidity of tree growth it may be assumed that trees growing at the *average* rate grow approximately 305 mm (1 ft) a year. In other words a tree with a potential 30.5 m (100 ft) will take a century, more or less, to reach that height. *A quick* growing tree would do it in two thirds of the time, say 457 mm (18 in) per year. *A very quick* tree may grow at twice the average rate, say 610 mm (2 ft) per year. *Slow growers* on the other hand would take a third as long again as the average, say 229 mm (9 in) a year while *very slow growers* would take twice as long as the average, say 152 mm (6 in) a year.

Taking all this as read, what is the choice? Either to be long-minded (and I would say somewhat unimaginative) and plant a tree of average growth rate and wait some time for results or to plant for immediate, reasonably quick results and for long-term (the grandchildrens') effect, coincidentally. That would mean investing in some large trees which will look like trees as soon as planted (expensive) or choosing some very quick growing trees of ordinary size and coincidentally, inter-planting some of average or slow growth 'to follow on', later removing the former.

Growth rate affects strength. Generally speaking the quicker a tree grows the weaker its structure and the sooner it dies! This suggests that quick growing trees are for temporary effect; other things being equal such would be the case. But growth rate is strongly influenced by the fertility of the soil and suitability of the climate. When these factors are sufficiently favourable a quick growing tree would rapidly out-grow its strength, crack, split, shed limbs and be damaged by storms, whereas in less favourable conditions, as when used as a pioneer on wasteland for example it would reach satisfactory maturity in a reasonable time.

Growth rate and strength are also affected by siting. If trees are planted too close together *and not appropriately thinned*, growth is drawn up (in competition for light), weak and subject to storm damage. This is a forestry problem and appropriate sources should be consulted (see Bibliography). With certain exceptions, e.g. the lamented elms which are notorious for unexpectedly shedding limbs, it will be found that correct ecological choice of species obviates such handicaps. That is why it is so important to check across all the columns of the tables to ensure that the tree selected has *all* its complementary requirements satisfied.

SOIL

What of the soil the tree is to grow in? Is it heavy (clay) or light (sand) or a friendly medium loam? Is it wet or dry, acid or alkaline or poisoned? These factors are vital.

Many trees will grow satisfactorily in either clay, sand or loam, while definitely preferring one or another. For clay soils trees which like growing in clay should be chosen and the same applies to sandy soils; if the soil is medium loam, the choice is wider. Some trees will grow on sand dunes and others in marshland, which they may drain in time through excess transpiration. Sandy soils in areas of light rainfall may need irrigation whereas marshes may need to be surface drained before planting.

Acid soils can be limed to improve their usefulness for growing plants whereas there is little that can be done to alkaline soils which would make them acceptable to lime-hating trees, whose roots penetrate to below the depth of cultivation.

Suiting trees to the soils to which they are naturally adapted – correct ecological choice in its truest sense – will reap the best results. In this way the planter goes along with nature and will be rewarded accordingly.

If actual pollution is suspected in the soil, confirmation should be obtained from a soil chemist. Some pollutants, copper, lead and salt for example, inhibit the growth of plants and can be dangerous and difficult, even virtually impossible, to deal with. Certainly expert advice would be needed before a decision to plant is taken.

POSITION

Where is the tree to go? In a shady, sunny, sheltered or open or exposed position? These factors must also influence choice.

ATMOSPHERIC TOLERANCE

What is the state of the atmosphere? Is the air pure? Is it salt laden or polluted with smoke or sulphur dioxide (SO_2)? Is the site a frosty one or exposed to winds or draughts? What is the rainfall? Is there likelihood of seasonal drought?

Winds blowing over the sea are salt laden and only a limited range of plants will tolerate such atmospheric pollution. Even along motorways spray borne salt, resulting from de-icing practices inhibits the growth of plants near the carriageway. Belts of trees tolerant of airborne salt can be established (with difficulty) to enable less tolerant species to thrive in their shelter.

A limited number of trees, London plane for example, will tolerate smoke, fewer are only somewhat tolerant of SO_2. But even combinations of salt and SO_2 pollution can be successfully overcome, as at the coastal industrial installation at Fawley on Southampton Water and elsewhere.

Some sites are frost pockets where topographical features prevent the free flow of cold air down slopes which chiefly occurs at night. Cold air being heavier than warm air, flows like water over the land. If it is held up by natural land forms or by buildings, as at the University of Essex, or by an embankment, e.g. by the railway crossing the valley at Rickmansworth (where the air temperature at night rarely exceeds freezing point!) the cold air builds up behind it, as water is held up by a dam, and forms a frost pocket which stretches up the contours to the height of the obstruction, over which it can then flow away. This frosty air is slow to clear in the morning. Young leaves and blossoms, of otherwise hardy trees are thus damaged, leading to failure of the full potential of the tree concerned.

If a topographical feature is noticed which looks as though it might hold up the free movement of air (as a dam across a valley holds up water) it is wise to seek expert climatological advice before spending money on planting unsuitable trees.

If a site is exposed to hostile, i.e. northerly or easterly, winds it is wise to select a tree which will tolerate exposure, e.g. Sycamore or Pine.

It is particularly difficult for a tree to withstand draughts between buildings and it may be necessary to build architectural artefacts to shelter trees in such situations.

It is worth taking particular care to ascertain rainfall and drought patterns so as to make sure that site conditions will satisfy the tree's needs, after contract maintenance is completed. (Trees may be cosseted by watering etc. during the contract maintenance period!). This is yet another example of the need to ensure ecological suitability in the choice of species.

PLANTING DISTANCES

These depend on the thoughts of the designer when making the planting plan; the trees would be disposed so as to express the underlying concepts of the design. When planted as specimens, such as trees in an arboretum, space must be alloted to each tree for it to grow to its best advantage. This space is determined by the height and mass (form) of the tree and determines the distance for planting surrounding trees. This distance is described as the 'ultimate spacing in metres (USM for short). The word 'ultimate' is used because, not infrequently, some quicker growing trees may be planted in-between, in order to improve the microclimate for healthy establishment and earlier effect, and later removed. The USM given is the minimum spacing for amenity planting when a tree is to be adjacent to one of similar species. If species are to be mixed, then the distance for planting should be determined by adding half the USM of the tree concerned to half the USM of its neighbour, thus if a broad spreading tree with USM 20 m is to be placed next to a columnar tree with USM 8 m then the planting distance between the two would be

$$\frac{20}{2} + \frac{8}{2} \, \text{USM} = 14 \, \text{m}.$$

←   20 m   →   ←   14 m   →   ←   8 m   →

USM

(Many early plantings are over crowded because the vital statistics, determining the USM, of exotics in particular were not known at the time of their introduction.)

NOTES

Finally trees have individual characteristics, inherent physiological qualities and intolerances. Many of the trees listed, being somewhat frost tender, are not hardy all over the British Isles. These, listed as giving full performance only in the south and west would be happy in districts warmed by the Gulf Stream and comparatively frost free. Elsewhere they might, in normal British winters, be risked in a southern aspect, protected from north and east winds. Similarly some trees may have special cultural or management needs, etc. so these are also mentioned.

ALL THIS DETAIL

Much detail must, in fact, be collected in search of the correct answer; so for clarity it is assembled in tabular form. *All* the trees' needs must be provided for correctly in order to avoid the mistakes which have led to the embarrassments and butchery as seen in obligatory felling and unnecessary lopping or the sad spectacle of unhealthy, dying trees.

Correct choice

Correct choice in the selection of a tree is the surest way of avoiding subsequent management problems. It ensures that the tree planted is ecologically adapted to the site it is to occupy; it will grow along with nature and so contribute to the biological balance prevailing in that place, while adding its own unique beauty and attraction to the site.

How to use the tables

There are two sections:

    I for large trees which normally grow taller than 15.24 m (50 ft);
    II for small trees which do not usually reach that height.

Within these sections trees are grouped according to their main colour, shape and leaf retention. The various shapes of large and small trees are indicated by the symbols shown below. Throughout the book a grey symbol indicates deciduous and a black symbol evergreen. The shape of the symbol against each entry in the tables shows at a glance the category to which the tree most nearly conforms.

MAIN COLOUR

(See colour plate section.)

Dark green
Light green
Yellow green green with yellow
             overtones.
Grey green   green with silvery
             overtones.
Blue green   green with blue overtones.
Red green   green with red overtones.
Blue grey   blue with silver overtones.
Yellow   golden foliage.
Blue   blue foliage.
Silver   silver foliage.
Red   red/purple foliage.

SHAPE

Deciduous	*Profiles*	*Evergreen*
	Broad spread growing wider than high and of no special shape	
	Narrow spread growing taller than broad and of no special shape	
	Conical roughly the shape of a broad cone	
	Spired the shape of a finely tapering spire	
	Columnar roughly the same width all the way up	
	Ovoid shape of an ovoid with ascending branches	
	Weeping branches generally weeping	

NOMENCLATURE

Both the Latin and common English names are given according to W. J. Bean's *Trees and Shrubs Hardy in the British Isles*, 8th edn (1970–80), with reference also to W. Dallimore and A. B. Jackson's *Handbook of Coniferae and Ginkgoaceae*, 4th edn (1974), and H. G. Hillier's *Manual of Trees and Shrubs* (1972).

Details of nomenclature follow those of W. J. Bean, *Trees and Shrubs Hardy to the British Isles*, in the 8th Revised Edition mentioned above. A complicated hierarchy governs the naming of plants, suffice it to note:

> The terms species and subspecies are the same in the singular and plural.
> *var.* denotes *varietas* (botanical variety; plural *varietates*)
> f. denotes *forma* (botanical form; plural *formae*)
> A name given in inverted commas indicates a cultivar (cv.) (garden variety or

form), cultivars of woody species are usually 'clones' composed of individuals descended asexually from a single ancestor by vegetative propagation and therefore identical.

Symbols by the species name: *, generally regarded as an indigenous species; Ø, in author's view has excellent qualities.

Page number shown in brackets where illustration is provided.

Where English names are not found in these sources, reference is to Alan Mitchell's *A Field Guide to the Trees of Britain and Northern Europe* or, fancifully by the author, with reference to other books listed in the bibliography.

OTHER COLUMN HEADINGS

A tree's suitability to provide shelter, form satisfactory backgrounds (as part of the framework of planting in a landscape), or as an individual element in the design is suggested in the column headed 'Siting', together with any special unique quality in display of leaf, flower, fruit or seasonal colour, etc. Details of leaf density, reflection, and texture follow, with growth rate, under the heading 'Growth'.

Environmental factors are then dealt with under successive headings: 'Soil Preference', 'Position', 'Air and soil tolerance', 'USM' (planting distances), with finally 'Notes' on inherent physiological qualities of the tree concerned, individual requirements, cultural needs and management advice.

So, by scanning across and down the columns, a list of trees to satisfy the requirements of the design and site can be quickly assembled.

Indexes of both Latin and common names are provided.

DARK GREEN
Ilex aquifolium
Holly

YELLOW GREEN
Chamaecyparis lawsoniana 'Lutea'
Golden Lawson Cypress

LIGHT GREEN
Thuga occidentalis
White Cedar

GREY GREEN
Abies pinsapo
Spanish Fir

BLUE GREEN
Juniperus squamata 'Blue Carpet'
Flaky Juniper

RED GREEN
Fagus sylvatica 'Cuprea'
Copper Beech

BLUE GREY
Picea pungens f. *glauca*
Colorado Spruce

YELLOW
Robinia pseudoacacia 'Frisia'
Golden False Acacia

BLUE
Picea pungens 'Koster'
Koster's Blue Spruce

SILVER
Hippophae rhamnoides
Sea Buckthorn

RED
Acer palmatum
'Atropurpureum'
Purple Japanese Maple

TABLES

LARGE TREES   *Growth*

Dark green	*Name*	*Siting and display*	*Density, reflection, surface pattern*	*Rate*
	Acer pseudoplatanus★ Sycamore (p. 18)	Shelter, background, fine as specimen; growth sculptural and cumulous giving deep shadows; grey scaling bark	Dense, matt, mottled	Quick
	Aesculus hippocastanum Horse-chestnut (p. 19)	Specimen; white flowers in May; bold foliage	Dense, matt, striated	Average
	*Aesculus indica*⁰ Indian Horse-chestnut	Specimen; bold foliage; silvery leaf reverses give lively effect; white flowers June–July	Dense, shiny, striated	Average
	Ailanthus altissima Tree of Heaven	Specimen; bold foliage, enlivened by pale underleaves; red-brown fruits in late summer, autumn colour	Dense, matt, feathery	Quick
	Cedrus libani Cedar of Lebanon (p. 26)	Specimen; throws out huge horizontal branches; growth in delicate layers gives strong light and shade	Open, matt, scaly	Average
	Pinus bungeana Lace-bark Pine	Specimen; very decorative bark, yellow and green, eventually white; brushed foliage gives a rough nap	Loose, matt, spiky	Slow
	Pinus densiflora Japanese Red Pine	Specimen; flat-topped growth in horizontal fans	Loose, matt, quilled	Average

★ Generally regarded as an indigenous species.
⁰ In author's view has excellent qualities.

Environment

| Soil preference | Position | Tolerance | | Ultimate spacing in metres | Notes |
		Air	Soil		
Loams, clay	Any but deep shade	Withstands wind, salt and SO_2; cold districts	Tolerant of lime and wasteland	18	Very hardy; foliage subject to fungal attack, becomes unsightly and secretion of honeydew renders it unsuitable for frequented sites; good bee tree; full performance in cooler parts
Loams	Sun or semi-shade	Dislikes over-exposure; smoke tolerant	Lime tolerant; wet or dry	20	Not suitable for very cold districts; good bee tree
Loams	Sun or semi-shade	Dislikes over-exposure; smoke tolerant	Lime tolerant	16	Not suitable for very cold districts; good bee tree
Light loams, clay	Sun, sheltered	Dislikes over-exposure; smoke tolerant	Lime tolerant	20	In towns plant females only; males smell; young plants have leaves up to 1.2 m (4 ft) long; good bee tree; full performance in south
Deep sandy loams, clay	Open	Suffers from weight of snow; low rainfall; smoke tolerant	Lime tolerant	20	Specimens should be planted young 1.2–1.8 m (4–6 ft) high to develop naturally; full performance only in south
Well-drained loams	Open	Endures exposure		8	Resents root disturbance; young pot-grown or regularly transplanted trees should be planted carefully; by inducing habit to throw many trunks this pine may be kept smaller
Well-drained loams	Open			8	Resents root disturbance; young pot-grown or regularly transplanted trees should be planted carefully; by inducing habit to throw many trunks this pine may be kept smaller

LARGE TREES

Dark green	Name	Siting and display	Growth Density, reflection, surface pattern	Rate
	*Prunus sargentii*⁰ Sargent's Cherry (p. 20)	Specimen; upstanding branch pattern; bronzy young foliage; superb pink flowers April; blazing autumn colour red yellow	Loose, matt, striated	Average
	*Quercus coccinea*⁰ Scarlet Oak	Background, specimen; bold foliage; blazing autumn colour, red, lasting for weeks often into December	Loose, shiny, curly	Average
	Quercus ilex Holm Oak (p. 21)	Background, specimen; growth cumulus and cascading	Dense, shiny, striated	Slow
	Quercus ilex 'Genabii' Genabi's Holm Oak	Specimen; bold foliage, leaves 13 cm (5 ins) long	Loose, shiny, striated	Slow
	*Quercus velutina*⁰ 'Rubrifolia' Champion's Black Oak	Specimen; enormous leaves up to 38 cm (15 ins) long, hanging lax, giving a liquid effect	Loose, shiny, striated	Average
	Robinia pseudoacacia False Acacia (p. 26)	Specimen; branches somewhat tortuous; white flowers in June	Loose, matt, woolly	Quick
	Robinia × ambigua 'Decaisneana' Decaisne's False Acacia	Specimen; branches somewhat tortuous; rose-red flowers in June	Loose, matt, woolly	Quick

Environment

Soil preference	Position	Tolerance		Ultimate spacing in metres	Notes
		Air	Soil		
Loams	Open, sun	Smoke tolerant	Lime tolerant	16	Cherries are shallow rooting and should not be planted deep, consequently staking is necessary
Loams, clay	Sheltered	Smoke tolerant		18	Oaks resent root disturbance; regularly transplanted trees should be planted carefully
Loams, clay	Open, sun	Withstands wind, salt, SO_2 and smoke; somewhat frost tender; milder districts	Drought and lime tolerant but dislikes pH extremes	16	Resents root disturbance; best planted very young from pots; May or September; unsightly litter of fallen leaves in summer is trapped by under-planting ivy or shade bearing shrubs; full performance in south and west
Well-drained loams, clay	Open, sun	Withstands wind, salt, SO_2 and smoke; somewhat frost tender; milder districts	Drought and lime tolerant but dislikes pH extremes	16	Resents root disturbance; best planted very young from pots; full performance in south and west
Loams	Any but shade	Dislikes over-exposure		18	Oaks resent root disturbance; regularly transplanted trees should be planted carefully
Poor or clay	Sheltered	Tolerates smoke, salt and some SO_2	Intolerant of pH extremes	14	Trees should be trained to a single leader to obviate splitting; suckers freely; fixes atmospheric nitrogen; pioneer species for tips and wasteland; good bee tree (see also p. 40)
Poor or clay	Sheltered	Tolerates smoke, salt and some SO_2	Lime tolerant	14	Trees should be trained to a single leader to obviate splitting; suckers freely; fixes atmospheric nitrogen; pioneer species for tips and wasteland; good bee tree

Acer pseudoplatanus
Sycamore

Aesculus hippocastanum
Horse-chestnut

Prunus sargent
Sargent's Cherr

Quercus ilex
Holm Oak

LARGE TREES

Dark green	Name	Siting and display	Growth Density, reflection, surface pattern	Rate
	Ulmus glabra★ Wych Elm	Shelter, background, specimen; fresh greenish-yellow flowers in spring; autumn colour yellow	Loose, matt, striated	Quick
Light green				
	Acer platanoides Norway Maple	Shelter, background, handsome as specimen; autumn colour red-yellow	Dense, shiny, mottled	Very quick
	Castanea sativa Spanish Chestnut (p. 28)	Specimen; prominent trunk with twist to the bark; cumulus growth	Dense, shiny, striated	Average
	Fagus sylvatica★ Beech (p. 29)	Background, specimen; silver-grey bark; stately tree with effect of frothy lightness; autumn colour brown	Dense, shiny, pitted	Average
	Fraxinus excelsior★ Ash (p. 36)	Background, specimen; pale grey, fissured bark; fine fruits in winter; has graceful drooping branchlets	Loose, matt, feathery	Quick
	Fraxinus excelsior★◊ f. *angustifolia* Fine-leafed Ash	Specimen; leaves shining silver; very fine lacey, feathery effect	Loose, shiny, fluffy	Quick
	Fraxinus ornus Manna Ash	Specimen; bold foliage; fine white flowers in May	Dense, matt, feathery	Quick
	Juglans nigra Black Walnut	Specimen; fine black bark, bold, fragrant foliage; leaves 60 cm (2 ft) long	Open, shiny, feathery	Average
	Juglans regia Common Walnut (p. 37)	Specimen; young shoots bronze in spring; edible nuts	Open, shiny, coarsely feathery	Average

Environment

Soil preference	Position	Tolerance		Ultimate spacing in metres	Notes
		Air	Soil		
Clay	Any but shade	Withstands wind, salt, smoke and some SO_2	Lime tolerant	18	Does best in cooler northern and western parts of the country
Any	Any but shade	Withstands wind; smoke and salt tolerant	Lime tolerant	18	Hardy and very vigorous; good bee tree
Hot dry, loams, sands	Sun	Dislikes over-exposure; good SO_2 resistance	Resists drought; acid tolerant	20	Full performance in south; good bee tree
Loams	Any	Dislikes over-exposure	Lime loving	20	Best planted young
Moist loams, clay	Any but shade	Withstands wind, smoke, salt and some SO_2	Lime loving	18	Gross feeder; transplants well
Moist loams, clay	Any but shade	Withstands wind, smoke, salt and SO_2	Lime loving	14	Gross feeder; transplants well
Moist loams	Any but shade	Salt, smoke tolerant	Lime tolerant	14	Flower scent unpleasant but faint
Clay	Sun	Dislikes over-exposure. Tolerates smoke	Lime loving	18	Plant young
Loams, clay	Sun	Dislikes over-exposure		18	For nuts, selected varieties should be chosen; plant young; full performance in south

LARGE TREES

| Light green | Name | Siting and display | Growth |||
			Density, reflection, surface pattern	Rate
	Pinus muricata Bishop Pine	Specimen; horizontal drooping habit gives a lovely sweep to growth	Loose, matt, quilled	Quick
	Platanus × acerifolia London Plane (p. 38)	Background, specimen; branches swirled; fine peeling bark; spherical fruits in winter	Loose, shiny, mottled	Quick
	Populus nigra Black Poplar (p. 39)	Background, specimen; purple-black bark; a tree of lively effect	Dense, matt, faceted	Quick
	Prunus avium★ Gean	Specimen; shiny peeling bark, white flowers April–May; blazing autumn colour red-yellow	Open, matt, striated	Quick
	Prunus avium★ 'Plena' Double Gean	Specimen; shiny peeling bark; magnificent double white flowers April–May; autumn colour red-yellow	Open, matt, striated	Average
	Prunus padus★⓪ 'Watereri' Bird Cherry	Specimen; strongly scented, clustered white flowers in May	Open, matt, striated	Average
	Quercus robur★ English Oak (p. 27)	Background, specimen; has a rugged, cumulus aspect; autumn colour russet	Loose, matt, curly	Slow

Environment

| Soil preference | Position | Tolerance | | Ultimate spacing in metres | Notes |
		Air	Soil		
Well-drained loams, sands	Any but shade	Withstands wind, salt and some SO_2; mild districts		14	Resents root disturbance; young pot-grown or regularly transplanted trees should be planted carefully
Loams, clay	Any but shade	Smoke, salt and SO_2 tolerant	Lime tolerant	18	
Moist loams, clay	Any but shade	Withstands wind, salt and smoke	Lime tolerant	20	Inadvisable to plant near buildings; this tree is now rare and substituted by varieties
Loams, clay	Any but deep shade	Smoke and salt tolerant	Lime and drought tolerant	16	Cherries are shallow rooting and should not be planted deep, consequently staking is necessary; good bee tree
Loams	Any but deep shade	Smoke and salt tolerant	Lime and drought tolerant	16	Cherries are shallow rooting and should not be planted deep, consequently staking is necessary
Loams, clay	Any but deep shade	Smoke and salt tolerant; cool districts	Lime and drought tolerant	14	Cherries are shallow rooting and should not be planted deep, consequently staking is necessary; performs magnificently in the North; good bee tree
Deep loams, clay	Any but shade	Withstands wind, salt and some SO_2	Dislikes pH extremes	20	Oaks resent root disturbance; regularly transplanted trees should be planted carefully

Cedrus libani
Cedar of Lebanon

Robinia pseudoacacia
False Acacia (type)

Quercus robur
English Oak

Paulownia tomentosa
(induced form)
Foxglove Tree

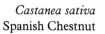

Castanea sativa
Spanish Chestnut

Fagus sylvatica
Beech

LARGE TREES

Light green	Name	Siting and display	Growth Density, reflection, surface pattern	Rate
	*Salix alba*⁰ 'Britzensis' Red-stemmed Willow	Background, specimen; splendid scarlet bark in winter	Loose, matt, striated	Quick
	*Salix alba*⁰ 'Vitellina' Yellow-stemmed White Willow	Background, specimen; beautiful yellow bark in winter	Loose, matt, striated	Quick
	*Sophora japonica*⁰ Pagoda Tree (p. 44)	Specimen; fine feathery, Mimosa like foliage, for warm clime effect; cream flowers in September	Loose, matt, smoky	Average
	Sorbus domestica Service Tree (p. 45)	Specimen; fine scaling bark; white flowers in May; green-brown fruits and good colour in autumn	Loose, matt, feathery	Slow
	Tsuga canadensis Canadian Hemlock	Specimen; may branch to form many trunks	Loose, shiny, striated	Quick
Grey green				
	Acer rubrum Red Maple (p. 46)	Specimen; grey under-leaves turn yellow-red in autumn (sometimes)	Loose, matt, mottled	Average
	Acer saccharinum Silver Maple	Specimen; foliage pendulous; white under leaves give dappled, lively effect; autumn colour yellow-red	Loose, matt, mottled	Quick

Environment

Soil preference	Position	Tolerance		Ultimate spacing in metres	Notes
		Air	Soil		
Wet or clay	Any but shade	Smoke and somewhat salt tolerant	Lime tolerant	14	Plant large cuttings broomstick size November–March or trees less than three years old, *deeper* than before; hammer in 30 cm (12 ins) lengths in populous places; best bark colour obtained by pruning hard every spring; good bee tree
Wet or clay	Any but shade	Smoke and somewhat salt tolerant	Lime tolerant	14	Plant large cuttings broomstick size November–March or trees less than three years old, *deeper* than before; hammer in 30 cm (12 ins) lengths in populous places; best bark colour obtained by pruning hard every spring; good bee tree
Loams	Sheltered, sun		Lime tolerant	14	Very fine tree, preferable to *Robinia* for good positions; good bee tree
Loams, clay or sand	Any but shade	Smoke tolerant	Lime tolerant	14	Young trees transplant best; a tree of average size
Moist clay or sand	Any	Withstands exposure	High rainfall	20	Detests dry conditions
Moist loams	Open, sun		Lime tolerant	18	Vigorous and free; good bee tree
Clay	Open	Salt and smoke tolerant	Lime tolerant	18	Vigorous and free; good bee tree

LARGE TREES

Grey green	Name	Siting and display	Growth Density, reflection, surface pattern	Rate
	Acer saccharinum⦿ f. *laciniatum* Cut-leafed Silver Maple	Specimen; silver under leaves give graceful, lively effect; drooping habit; autumn colour yellow-red	Loose, matt, feathery	Quick
	Fagus sylvatica★ f. *laciniata* Fern-leafed Beech	Specimen; finely divided leaves give frothing, feathery effect; autumn colour brown	Dense, matt, fluffy	Average
	Pinus montezumae Montezuma Pine	Specimen; long, bold needles brushed into rosettes give deep shaggy nap and smoky appearance	Loose, shiny, quilled	Average
	Pinus pinea Stone Pine (p. 47)	Specimen; becomes flat-topped; fine orange-brown bark deeply fissured	Dense (topped) matt, bristly	Average
	Prunus × *yedoensis* Yoshino Cherry	Specimen; fragrant, blush flowers March–April	Loose, matt, striated	Average
	Quercus × *hispanica* 'Lucombeana' Lucombe Oak	Specimen, bright foliage; cumulous growth, lively and lax	Loose, shiny, curly	Average
	Quercus petraea★ Durmast Oak (p. 52)	Background, specimen; black bark, airy effect; autumn colour russet	Loose, shiny, curly	Average
	Salix fragilis★ Crack Willow (p. 53)	Background; boldly corrugated bark	Loose, matt, striated	Quick

Environment

Soil preference	Position	Tolerance		Ultimate spacing in metres	Notes
		Air	Soil		
Clay	Open	Salt and smoke tolerant	Lime tolerant	18	Good near water; good bee tree
Sandy loams	Sheltered	Dislikes over-exposure	Lime loving	20	Best planted young
Well-drained loams	Sheltered	Frost tender; mild districts		14	
Well-drained loams	Open	Frost tender; mild districts	Lime tolerant	14	Only youngest trees will transplant; may need some protection at first
Loams	Open	Smoke tolerant	Lime tolerant	18	Cherries are surface rooting and should not be planted deep, consequently staking is necessary; good bee tree
Deep loams, clay	Any but shade	Somewhat frost tender; withstands salt and smoke	Drought tolerant; dislikes pH extremes	20	Oaks resent root disturbance; regularly transplanted trees should be planted carefully; only semi-evergreen under adverse conditions
Sandy loams, clay	Any but shade	Withstands wind and salt; high elevations	High rainfall; dislikes pH extremes	20	Oak resents root disturbance; regularly transplanted trees should be planted carefully; grows narrower with age
Wet loams, clay	Any but shade	Withstands exposure	Lime tolerant	14	Plant large cuttings broomstick size, November–March or trees less than three years old, *deeper* than before; hammer in 30 cm (12 ins) lengths in populous places; for quick, temporary effect

LARGE TREES

Blue grey	Name	Siting and display	Growth — Density, reflection, surface pattern	Rate
	Pinus pinaster Maritime Pine	Shelter, seaside specimen; umbrella shaped head; fine orange-brown bark deeply fissured	Loose, matt, quilled	Very quick
Silver				
	Salix alba★⁰ f. *argentea* Silver Willow	Background, specimen; fine silvery-white foliage	Loose, matt, striated	Average
Red green				
	Acer platanoides 'Schwedleri' Copper Norway Maple	Shelter, background, specimen; spring and autumn colour red	Loose, shiny, mottled	Quick
	Acer pseudoplatanus★⁰ 'Atropurpureum' Copper Sycamore	Shelter, background, specimen; dark green leaves purple underneath, neat habit	Dense, shiny, mottled	Quick
	Fagus sylvatica★ 'Cuprea' Copper Beech	Background, specimen; stately, frothy effect	Dense, shiny, pitted	Average
Yellow				
	*Acer mono*⁰ 'Marmoratum' Golden Mono Maple	Specimen; white dusted, yellow leaves	Loose, matt, mottled	Average

Environment

Soil preference	Position	Tolerance		Ultimate spacing in metres	Notes
		Air	Soil		
Sands	Any but shade	Withstands wind, salt and some SO_2; frost tender	Drought tolerant	8	Only youngest trees transplant; large groups are best sown direct; full performance only in south and west
Wet or clay	Any but shade	Wind and smoke tolerant	Lime tolerant	14	Plant large cuttings broomstick size November–March or trees less than three years old *deeper* than before; hammer in 30 cm (12 ins) lengths in populous places; good bee tree
Loams	Any but shade	Withstands wind and salt	Lime tolerant	18	Very hardy; good bee tree
Poor moist loams	Any but shade	Withstands wind, salt, smoke and some SO_2; cold districts	Lime tolerant	18	Very hardy; foliage, subject to fungal attack, becomes unsightly and secretion of honeydew renders it unsuitable for frequented sites; good for tips and wasteland; good bee tree
Sandy loams	Any	Dislikes over-exposure	Lime loving	20	Best planted young
Loams, clay	Any but shade		Lime tolerant	18	Vigorous and free; select for colour; good bee tree

Fraxinus excelsior
Ash

Juglans regia
Common Walnut

38

Populus nigra
Black Poplar

LARGE TREES

Yellow	Name	Siting and display	Growth Density, reflection, surface pattern	Rate
	Acer pseudoplatanus★ 'Corstorphinense' Corstorphine Sycamore f. variegatum	Background, specimen for bleak sites Is blotched yellow-green	Dense, matt, mottled	Quick
	Fraxinus excelsior★ 'Aurea' Golden Ash	Specimen; prominent, fissured, warm-grey trunk and yellow twigs in winter; swirled growth of branches gives effect of grace and movement	Loose, shiny, feathery	Slow
	Robinia pseudoacacia 'Frisia' Golden False Acacia (p. 54)	Specimen; brilliant golden foliage. White flowers in June	Loose, matt, woolly	Quick
Red				
	Acer platanoides 'Goldsworth Purple' Red Norway Maple	Background; fine specimen	Loose, shiny, mottled	Quick
	Fagus sylvatica★ f. purpurea Purple Beech	Background, specimen; stately, frothy effect	Dense, shiny, pitted	Average
Dark green				
	Aesculus × carnea Red Horse-chestnut	Specimen; red flowers in May; bold foliage	Dense, matt, curly	Average
	Araucaria araucana Monkey Puzzle (p. 55)	Specimen; horizontal fans of bold snakey growth in regular tiers	Loose, shiny, scaly	Average

Environment

Soil preference	Position	Tolerance Air	Soil	Ultimate spacing in metres	Notes
Poor moist loams	Any but deep shade	Withstands wind, salt, smoke and SO₂; cold districts	Lime tolerant	18	Foliage subject to fungal attack, becomes unsightly and secretion of honeydew renders it unsuitable for frequented sites; good for tips and wasteland
Moist loams, clay	Any but shade	Withstands wind, smoke, some salt and SO₂	Lime loving	16	Gross feeder, transplants well; good bee tree
Poor or clay	Sheltered	Tolerates smoke, salt and some SO₂	Intolerant of pH extremes	14	Trees should be trained to a single leader to obviate splitting; suckers freely; pioneer species for tips and wasteland; good bee tree
Loams	Any but shade	Withstands wind and salt	Lime tolerant	18	Hardy and vigorous; good bee tree
Sandy loams	Any	Dislikes over-exposure	Lime loving	20	Best planted young
Dry or moist loams	Sun or semi-shade	Smoke tolerant, dislikes over-exposure	Lime tolerant	16	Not suitable for very cold districts; good bee tree
Clay	Open	Somewhat frost tender; mild districts	High rainfall	14	Young trees have sculptural grace; mature ones are beautiful only when grown in conditions suitable to perfect development

LARGE TREES

Dark green	Name	Siting and display	Growth Density, reflection, surface pattern	Rate
	*Betula platyphylla*⁰ var. *szechuanica* Szechwan Birch	Specimen; black twigs contrasting with superb white bark; light under-leaves give dappled effect	Open, shiny, striated	Quick
	Carpinus betulus★ Hornbeam (p. 60)	Shelter, background, specimen; graceful growth, fine fluted bark; autumn colour yellow	Loose, matt, pitted	Average
	Juniperus virginiana Red Cedar	Specimen; columnar when young, growth somewhat rugged	Loose, matt, mossy	Slow
	*Nothofagus dombeyi*⁰ Dombey's Southern Beech (p. 61)	Specimen; branches assurgent; lovely swirled growth	Loose, shiny, feathery	Quick
	Pinus nigra Austrian Pine (p. 62)	Shelter, background; warm-brown bark, streaked fawn	Loose, matt, quilled	Quick
	Pinus nigra var. *maritima* Corsican Pine	Shelter, specimen; coarse growth	Loose, matt, quilled	Quick
	Pinus radiata Monterey Pine	Background, specimen; rich, bright foliage	Dense, shiny, quilled	Very quick
	Pinus rigida Northern Pitch Pine	Temporary specimen; light powdering of thin branches with feathery rosettes of foliage gives a gnarled look	Open, matt, quilled	Quick

Environment

| Soil preference | Position | Tolerance | | Ultimate spacing in metres | Notes |
		Air	Soil		
Loams	Open		Lime tolerant	14	Transplants badly, very young trees should be chosen
Loams, heavy clay	Any	Withstands wind	Lime tolerant	16	Very hardy; makes good hedges
Loams	Any but shade		Lime loving	8	Young trees transplant
Clay	Sheltered		High rainfall	14	May lose its foliage in severe winters
Poor, dry	Any but shade	Withstands wind, smoke and salt	Highly lime tolerant	8	Useful only as a pioneer for poor chalky soils; resents root disturbance; young pot-grown or regularly transplanted trees should be planted carefully
Poor, including sand and peat	Any but shade	Withstands wind, salt and some SO_2 and smoke	Lime tolerant; drought resistant	8	Pioneer for bleak and maritime situations, outgrowing weeds; immune to rabbits; resents root disturbance; young pot-grown or regularly transplanted trees should be planted carefully
Well-drained loams, sands	Any but shade	Withstands wind and salt; frost tender; mild districts	Lime tolerant; drought tolerant	14	Resents root disturbance; young pot-grown or regularly transplanted trees should be planted carefully; full performance only in south and west
Loams	Any but shade	Withstands wind	Withstands drought; lime hating; thrives on poor soils	8	Resents root disturbance; young pot-grown or regularly transplanted trees should be planted carefully; sometimes does not live to maturity

44

Sophora japonica
Pagoda Tree

Sorbus domestica
Service Tree

46

Acer rubrum
Red Maple

Pinus Pinea
Stone Pine

LARGE TREES

Dark green	Name	Siting and display	Growth Density, reflection, surface pattern	Rate
	Populus trichocarpa Black Cottonwood	Shelter, background, specimen; yellow-grey bark; bold foliage on drooping black twigs; delightfully fragrant in spring	Loose, shiny, faceted	Quick
	Quercus cerris Turkey Oak	Background, specimen; good for avenues; lively foliage	Loose, shiny, striated	Quick
	Quercus pyrenaica Pyrenean Oak (p. 63)	Specimen; enlivened by white under-leaves in summer	Loose, shiny, feathery	Average
	Quercus rubra Red Oak	Background, specimen; boldly cut foliage; autumn colour russet	Loose, shiny, mottled	Quick
	*Tilia cordata*⁰ Small-leafed Lime (p. 68)	Background, specimen; black bark; delicate foliage in irregular drooping tiers; fragrant flowers in July	Loose, shiny, clotted	Slow
	Ulmus procera★ English Elm	Background; characteristic petticoat of foliage around trunk; lovely winter tracery of twigs; autumn colour yellow	Loose, matt, pitted	Average

Light green

| | *Betula albo-sinensis*⁰
Chinese Red-barked Birch
(p. 69) | Specimen; superb, glazed, dusty pink-brown bark, peeling in ragged papery layers; splendid winter effect | Loose, shiny, striated | Quick |

Environment

Soil preference	Position	Tolerance		Ultimate spacing in metres	Notes
		Air	Soil		
Moist, loams, clay	Any but shade	Withstands wind, salt SO$_2$ and smoke		20	Grows quickly from cuttings
Deep loams, clay	Any but shade	Resists smoke, salt and more than average exposure	Lime and drought tolerant	20	Oak resents root disturbance; regularly transplanted trees should be planted carefully
Loams	Open			20	Oak resents root disturbance; regularly transplanted trees should be planted carefully
Loams, clay	Any but shade	Smoke tolerant		18	Oak resents root disturbance; regularly transplanted trees should be planted carefully
Loams, clay	Any but shade	Withstands wind and smoke	Lime tolerant	16	Trees raised from seed should be chosen; the chief substitute for elm recommended by the Forestry Commission; good bee tree
Deep loams	Any	Resists smoke, salt; dislikes over-exposure	Lime tolerant	18	Sheds large limbs without warning and so is unsuitable for frequented sites; gross feeder and bad neighbour in south; subject to Dutch elm disease
Loams	Open		Lime tolerant	14	Transplants badly, very young trees should be chosen

LARGE TREES

Light green	Name	Siting and display	Growth Density, reflection, surface pattern	Rate
	Betula pendula★ Silver Birch	Shelter, specimen; orange-brown twigs contrasting with white bark in winter; foliage hangs in bunches from drooping twigs, giving light but langourous effect; autumn colour yellow	Loose, shiny, pitted	Quick
	Betula pubescens★ Downy Birch	Shelter, specimen; beautiful purple buds in winter; trunk becomes rugged	Loose, shiny, pitted	Quick
	Liquidambar styraciflua⊙ Sweet Gum (p. 70)	Specimen; in full leaf effect is smokey; autumn colour red and orange	Dense, matt, feathery	Average
	Liriodendron tulipifera Tulip Tree (p. 71)	Specimen; bold, handsome foliage, grey under-leaves give dappled effect; greenish-white flowers in June–July; autumn colour gold	Loose, shiny, mottled	Quick
	Populus × *canadensis* 'Robusta' Hybrid Black Poplar	Shelter, background; brilliant rich bronze young leaves and fine catkins in spring	Loose, shiny, faceted	Very quick
	Quercus robur★⊙ 'Filicifolia' Lacy-leafed Oak	Specimen; most elegant of oaks with delicate foliage	Open, matt, lacy	Slow

Yellow green

	Catalpa speciosa Western Catalpa	Specimen; bold handsome foliage; white flowers in July	Loose, matt, plumy	Average

Environment

Soil preference	Position	Tolerance		Ultimate spacing in metres	Notes
		Air	Soil		
Well-drained loams; poor sands, clay	Any but shade	Resists wind, salt smoke and some SO_2	Lime and acid tolerant; drought tolerant	14	Pioneer species for poor soils
Any	Any but shade	Resists wind and SO_2	Tolerant of lime and poor drainage; high altitudes	14	Transplants badly; very young trees should be chosen
Moist loams, clay	Any but shade	Warm, sheltered	Intolerant of drought and lime	14	A site not subject to late spring frost should be chosen
Deep loams, clay	Sun	Smoke tolerant	Lime tolerant	20	Plant young in May; good bee tree
Moist loams, clay	Any but shade	Smoke, SO_2 and salt		20	Valuable for shelter and quick effect; inadvisable to plant near buildings
Deep loams, clay	Any but shade	Stands salt and some SO_2	Dislikes pH extremes	18	Resents root disturbance; young trees should be planted carefully
Clay	Sheltered, sun	Stands salt and some SO_2	Dislikes lime	20	Splendid town tree; may need training in youth; full performance in south

Salix fragilis
Crack Willow

Robinia pseudoacacia 'Frisia'
Golden False Acaci

Araucaria araucana
Monkey Puzzle

LARGE TREES

Yellow green	Name	Siting and display	Growth Density, reflection, surface pattern	Rate
	*Gleditsia triacanthos*⁰ Honey Locust (p. 76)	Specimen; graceful, airy effect; autumn colour yellow	Loose, shiny, feathery	Slow
	Pinus sylvestris⋆⁰ 'Aurea' Golden Scots Pine	Background, specimen; foliage golden in winter	Loose, matt, bristly	Quick
	Populus × *canadensis* 'Serotina Aurea' Golden Poplar	Background, temporary specimen; spring and autumn colour gold; lively dappled effect	Loose, shiny, faceted	Very quick
Grey green				
	Alnus hirsuta Manchurian Alder	Specimen; branches prominent; dark fruits; has aged, gnarled look	Loose, matt, striated	Average
	Alnus incana Grey Alder	Shelter, background; conical in youth; autumn colour	Loose, matt, striated	Average
	*Alnus incana*⁰ 'Laciniata' Cut-leafed Grey Alder	Specimen; delicate foliage; gives light, woolly effect	Loose, matt, feathery	Average
	Alnus incana 'Ramulis Coccineis' Red-stemmed Grey Alder	Specimen; red catkin scales and twigs in winter and spring	Loose, matt, striated	Average
	Eucalyptus gunnii Cider Gum	Specimen; fine yellow-grey peeling bark, intensely delicate foliage shining silver, strong fragrance; for warm clime effect	Open, shiny, lacy	Quick

Environment

Soil preference	Position	Tolerance		Ultimate spacing in metres	Notes
		Air	*Soil*		
Sandy loams, clay	Sun	Smoke tolerant, SO_2 tolerant	Lime tolerant	14	Armed with formidable spines; full performance in south
Sandy loams	Any but shade	Withstands wind and some SO_2 and climatic extremes; cold districts	High rainfall; acid and lime tolerant	9	Useful for furnishing
Moist loams, clay	Any but shade	Smoke tolerant		20	For quick effect; inadvisable to plant near buildings
Moist loams, clay	Any but shade			14	Happiest near, but not in, water
Any wet or clay even slags	Any but shade	Survives cold; smoke tolerant	Lime tolerant	14	Pioneer for bleak situations; builds up soil fertility by fixing atmospheric nitrogen
Any wet or clay even slags	Any but shade	Survives cold; smoke tolerant	Lime tolerant	14	Invaluable for bleak situations, providing ornament where so little will grow
Any wet or clay even slags	Any but shade	Survives cold; smoke tolerant	Lime tolerant	14	Invaluable for bleak situations, providing ornament where so little will grow
Loams	Sheltered	Tolerates some salt and smoke; frost tender; mild districts		14	Young trees should be planted late in spring. Protection from frost for first few years makes establishment more certain; full performance in south and west

LARGE TREES

Grey green	Name	Siting and display	Growth — Density, reflection, surface pattern	Rate
	*Gleditsia triancanthos*⁰ 'Bujotii' Grey Honey Locust	Specimen; drooping branches with intensely fine and delicate foliage, shining silver in streaming tassels; autumn colour yellow	Open, shiny, lacy	Slow
	Pinus nigra var. *caramanica* Crimean Pine	Specimen, angular branching gives a waltzing effect	Loose, shiny, quilled	Quick
	Pinus sylvestris★⁰ Scots Pine (p. 77) 'Alba' White-needled Scots Pine	Shelter, background, specimen; fine orange-red and grey bark. Growth cumulus and streaming Is suffused with white, blossom-like young growths	Loose, matt, quilled	Quick
	Populus canescens★⁰ Grey Poplar (p. 78)	Background, specimen; bold branches sparsely clothed with leaves, enlivened by silver reverses; beautiful yellow-grey bark, finely marked black; almost sub-tropical effect	Open, shiny, frothy	Quick
	*Quercus frainetto*⁰ Hungarian Oak	Specimen; strikingly bold foliage – leaves up to 20 cm (8 ins) long	Loose	Slow
	Rhus verniciflua Varnish Tree	Specimen, bold handsome foliage and yellow flowers in autumn	Open, shiny, feathery	Average
	Salix alba 'Caerulea' Cricket-bat Willow	Background, specimen; neat, shapely head	Loose, matt, striated	Very quick

Environment

Soil preference	Position	Tolerance		Ultimate spacing in metres	Notes
		Air	Soil		
Sandy loams	Sheltered, sun	Smoke and SO_2 tolerant; somewhat frost tender		14	Of variable size; armed with formidable spines; full performance in south
Poor	Any but shade	Withstands wind	Lime tolerant; drought resisting	8	Pines resent root disturbance; young pot-grown or regularly transplanted trees should be planted carefully
Any well-drained	Any but shade	Withstands wind, some SO_2, salt and climatic extremes	Lime and acid tolerant; cold districts high rainfall	8	Pines resent root disturbance; young pot-grown or regularly transplanted trees should be planted carefully
Moist loams, or dry soils	Any but shade	Stands smoke, salt and SO_2	Dislikes pH extremes	20	Grows quickly from cuttings; suckers freely
Sandy loams, clay	Any but shade	Smoke tolerant; dislikes over-exposure		20	Oaks resent root disturbance; young trees should be planted carefully
Loams	Sun	Smoke and SO_2 tolerant	Lime tolerant	14	A tree of medium size
Moist or clay	Any but shade	Salt and smoke tolerant	Lime tolerant	18	Plant large cuttings broomstick size November–March or trees less than three years old, *deeper* than before; hammer in 30 cm (12 ins) lengths in populous places; good bee tree

Carpinus betul
Hornbea

Nothofagus dombeyi
Dombey's Southern Beech

Pinus nigra
Austrian Pine

Quercus pyrenaica
Pyrenean Oak

LARGE TREES

Grey green	Name	Siting and display	Growth — Density, reflection, surface pattern	Rate
	Sorbus torminalis★⊘ Wild Service Tree	Specimen; bold foliage; pale under leaves give fresh effect; brownish fruits and fine colour in autumn	Loose, shiny, feathery	Average
Blue grey				
	Pinus sylvestris★⊘ f. *argentea* Silver Scots Pine	Specimen; fine red and grey bark; growth cumulus and streaming	Loose, matt, bristly	Quick
Yellow				
	Alnus incana★ 'Aurea' Golden Grey Alder	Background, specimen; wholly yellow; red twigs and buds in winter and spring	Loose, matt, striated	Average
	Ulmus 'Louis Van Houtte' Golden Elm	Background; beautiful yellow foliage, persisting to autumn colour	Loose, matt, pitted	Average
Red				
	Betula pendula★ 'Purpurea' Purple Birch	Background, specimen; red foliage contrasting with silvery-red bark	Loose, shiny, pitted	Quick
Dark green				
	Abies firma Japanese Fir (p. 79)	Specimen; stiff, narrow fans in regular upturning tiers	Open, matt, mossy	Quick

Environment

Soil preference	Position	Tolerance		Ultimate spacing in metres	Notes
		Air	Soil		
Rich loams, clay	Any but shade		Lime tolerant	14	A tree of average size
Sandy loams	Any but shade	Withstands wind, some SO_2 and climatic extremes; cold districts	Lime and acid tolerant; high rainfall	8	Useful for furnishing bleak situations; resents root disturbance; young pot-grown or regularly transplanted trees should be planted carefully
Any wet or clay even slags	Any but shade	Survives cold, some SO_2 and smoke	Lime tolerant	14	Pioneer for bleak situations, builds up soil fertility by fixing atmospheric nitrogen
Deep loams		Resists smoke, salt, exposure	Lime loving	8	Sheds large limbs without warning and so is unsuitable for frequented sites; gross feeder and bad neighbour; full performance in south
Sandy loams, clay	Any but shade	Smoke and SO_2 tolerant	Acid tolerant	14	A medium sized tree
Loams	Any	Dislikes late spring frosts; cool districts; high rainfall	Lime hating	8	Young trees transplant best

LARGE TREES

Dark green	Name	Siting and display	Growth Density, reflection, surface pattern	Rate
	Alnus cordata Italian Alder (p. 84)	Specimen; enlivened by pale under-leaves	Loose, shiny, striated	Average
	Cedrus deodara Deodar	Specimen; elegant, pergoda like growth in tiers, delicate dependant branchlets; becomes flat-topped with age	Loose, matt, woolly	Average
	Chamaecyparis obtusa Hinoki Cypress	Specimen; graceful, neat habit furnished with foliage to the ground	Loose, matt, mottled	Slow
	*Corylus colurna*⁰ Turkish Hazel	Specimen; formal shape; handsome foliage	Dense, matt, striated	Slow
	*Cryptomeria japonica*⁰ Japanese Red Cedar (p. 85)	Specimen; clothed to the ground with foliage	Dense, matt, coarsely feathery	Quick
	Picea abies Norway Spruce	Background, specimen; clothed to ground with foliage, familar as Christmas trees	Loose, matt, bristly	Quick when established
	Pinus heldreichii var. *leucodermis* Bosnian Pine (p. 86)	Shelter, background, specimen	Loose, shiny, bristly	Quick
	Tilia platyphyllos 'Rubra' Red-twigged Lime	Specimen; red twigs; foliage lifeless	Loose, matt, clotted	Average

Environment

Soil preference	Position	Tolerance		Ultimate spacing in metres	Notes
		Air	Soil		
Wet or dry loams or clay	Any but shade	Stands wind and smoke	Lime tolerant	14	Best near water; pioneer species synthesizes its own nitrate
Deep loams, clay	Open	Frost tender; mild districts; tolerates some smoke	Lime tolerant	20	Specimens should be chosen for colour and planted young 1.2–1.8 m (4–6 ft) high, to develop naturally
Moist loams, clay	Open	High rainfall	Acid soils	8	Resents root disturbance; young pot-grown or regularly transplanted trees should be planted carefully
Loams	Any but shade	Climatic extremes	Lime tolerant	14	
Wet loams, clay	Sheltered	Mild districts; high rainfall	Intolerant of drought	8	Young trees transplant best
Loams, clay	Any	High altitudes; cold districts; high rainfall but dislikes over-exposure	Lime hating	8	Owing to slow early growth trees about six years old may be chosen; important to plant shallow
Poor	Any but shade	Withstands exposure; high altitudes	Lime loving	8	Young or pot-grown trees should be planted carefully
Loams, clay	Any but shade	Smoke and salt tolerant	Lime loving	16	Carefully propagated trees should be chosen; good bee tree

Tilia cordat
Small-leafed Lim

Betula albo-sinensis
Chinese Red-barked Birch

Liquidambar styraciflua
Sweet Gum

Liriodendron tulipifera
Tulip Tree

LARGE TREES

Dark green	Name	Siting and display	Density, reflection, surface pattern	Rate
	Tsuga heterophylla Western Hemlock	Specimen; perfect loose silhouette; fronded growth in broken tiers, clothed with mossy drapery to the ground	Loose, shiny, mossy	Quick
	Tsuga × jeffreyi Jeffrey's Hybrid Hemlock	Specimen; felted growth in upturned broken tiers	Loose, matt, mossy	Quick
	Tsuga mertensiana Mountain Hemlock	Specimen; fine silhouette; fronded growth in broken tiers clothes it to the ground	Dense, matt, mossy	Quick
Light green				
	*Betula nigra*⁰ River Birch (p. 87)	Specimen; contrasting dark bark; tends to assume coppice-like form	Loose shiny, pitted	Quick
	Castanea sativa 'Pyramidalis' Pyramidal Spanish Chestnut	Specimen; prominent trunk with a twist to the bark; full performance in south	Dense, shiny, striated	Slow
	Cedrus atlantica Atlas Cedar	Specimen; assurgent growth becomes layered in stiff horizontal fronds and flat-topped with age	Loose, matt, mossy	Average
	*Ginkgo biloba*⁰ Maidenhair Tree (p. 88)	Specimen; main limbs shooting and angular; drooping foliage gives fountain effect; autumn colour yellow	Loose, matt, pitted	Average

Environment

| Soil preference | Position | Tolerance | | Ultimate spacing in metres | Notes |
		Air	Soil		
Sandy loams, clay	Any	Intolerant of smoke	Fairly tolerant of dry conditions but not of lime	8	
Good loams	Any		High rainfall	8	Dislikes dry conditions
Clay	Any	Dislikes drought conditions; withstands exposure	High rainfall	8	Choose specimens for colour
Rich moist loams	Any but shade	Damp air	Temporary water logging	14	Transplants badly; young trees should be chosen
Hot, dry, loams, sands	Sun	Dislikes exposure; withstands salt, SO_2 and smoke	Survives drought	18	Trees grown from seed should be chosen; good bee tree
Loams, clay, sand	Open	Tolerates some salt, smoke and exposure	Lime tolerant; withstands drought	20	Specimens should be chosen for colour and planted young 1.2–1.8 m (4–6 ft) high to develop naturally
Loams, clay, sand	Sun; sheltered	Smoke tolerant	Lime tolerant	14	Unisexual, male trees tend to be more slender than female ones

LARGE TREES

Growth

Light green	Name	Siting and display	Density, reflection, surface pattern	Rate
	Picea polita Tiger-tail Spruce	Specimen; tall specimens clothed to ground with foliage, stiff growth becoming pendulous with age	Dense, shiny, bristly	Slow
	Ulmus × hollandica 'Belgica' Belgium Elm	Specimen; growth in umbrella shaped tiers; autumn colour yellow	Loose, matt, pitted	Quick

Yellow green

	Abies homolepis Nikko Fir	Specimen; horizontal tiered growth in shaggy spikes	Loose, matt, striated	Quick
	Cedrus deodara 'Aurea' Golden Deodar	Specimen; elegant layered growth; becomes flat-topped with age	Loose, matt, woolly	Average
	Cupressus macrocarpa 'Lutea' Golden Monterey Cypress	Background, specimen; growth upturned becomes spreading with age	Dense, matt, bristly	Quick
	Picea glauca 'Aurea' Golden spruce	Specimen, bleak situations; tiered growth	Open, matt, bristly	Quick when established

Environment

Soil reference	*Position*	*Tolerance* Air	Soil	*Ultimate spacing in metres*	*Notes*
Moist loams	Any	Dislikes over-exposure; high rainfall		8	Owing to slow early growth trees about six years old may be chosen; important to plant shallow
Loams, clay	Any but shade	Tolerates smoke and salt; withstands exposure	Lime tolerant	20	Young trees may require training
Loams, clay	Any	Cool districts; dislikes late spring frosts; tolerates some smoke and SO_2	Lime loving; fairly tolerant of drought	8	Young trees transplant best; very hardy
Loams, clay	Open	Frost tender; mild districts	Lime tolerant	16	Specimens should be chosen for colour and planted young 1.2–1.8 m (4–6 ft) high to develop naturally
Loams, clay	Any but shade	Salt tolerant; frost tender; mild districts	Lime tolerant	8	Resents root disturbance; young pot-grown or regularly transplanted trees should be planted carefully; may require protection at first; if clipped whole trees liable to die without warning; less liable to scorch than the type
Any	Any	Wind and salt tolerant; high altitudes; cold districts		8	Leaves evil smelling when crushed; owing to slow early growth trees about 6 years old should be planted carefully

Gleditsia triacantha
Honey Locus

Pinus sylvestris
Scots Pine

Populus canescens
Grey Poplar

Abies firma
Japanese Fir

LARGE TREES

Grey green	Name	Siting and display	Growth Density, reflection, surface pattern	Rate
	Abies pinsapo Spanish Fir	Specimen; growth in circling tiers	Loose, matt, scaly	Quick
	*Betula pendula*⁰ 'Dalecarlica' Dalecarlian Silver Birch	Specimen; very white trunk, cut leaves in pendant plumes give elegant and graceful effect	Loose, shiny, lacy	Quick
	*Cedrus atlantica*⁰ f. *glauca* Silver Atlas Cedar (p. 89)	Specimen; assurgent growth, becomes layered in stiff horizontal fronds, flat-topped with age	Loose, matt, mossy	Average
	Picea spinulosa Sikkim Spruce	Specimen; symmetrical form, streaming dependant branches	Loose, shiny, bristly	Quick when established
	Picea sitchensis Sitka Spruce	Background; specimens in groups; beautiful when mature	Loose, matt, bristly	Quick
	*Tilia tomentosa*⁰ 'Petiolaris' Silver Pendant Lime	Background, specimen; graceful drooping habit; silver under-leaves give lively effect; fragrant flowers July–August	Loose, shiny, clotted	Quick

Blue green

	*Abies pinsapo*⁰ f. *glauca* Blue Spanish Fir (p. 94)	Specimen; growth in circling tiers	Loose, matt, scaly	Quick

Environment

| Soil preference | Position | Tolerance | | Ultimate spacing in metres | Notes |
		Air	Soil		
Loams	Any	Dislikes late spring frost; cool districts; high rainfall	Lime tolerant	8	Young trees transplant best
Well-drained loams, poor sands, clay	Any but shade	Stands some SO_2 and smoke		14	Useful for furnishing arid situations
Loams	Open	Tolerates some salt and smoke	Lime tolerant; withstands drought	16	Specimens should be chosen for colour and planted young 1.2–1.8 m (4–6 ft) high to develop naturally
Moist loams	Any	Dislikes over-exposure; high rainfall		8	Owing to slow early growth trees about 6 years old may be planted shallow
Wet loams, clay	Any	Dislikes over-exposure	Lime hating; bogland or sandy	8	Very useful for furnishing bogs
Clay	Any but shade	Smoke tolerant	Lime loving	20	Narcotic and therefore unsuitable for bees
Loams	Any	Dislikes late spring frosts; cool districts; high rainfall	Lime tolerant	8	Young trees transplant best

LARGE TREES

Blue green	Name	Siting and display	Growth	
			Density, reflection, surface pattern	Rate
	Picea breweriana Brewer Spruce	Specimen; horizontal growth in tiers; very delicate hanging branchlets, depending, bearded plumes	Loose, shiny, plumy	Slow
	Picea likiangensis Likiang Spruce	Specimen; beautiful red-brown bark; outstanding red flowers in May	Dense, matt, plumy	Quick when established
Blue grey				
	Picea pungens f. *glauca* Blue Spruce	Specimen; stiff growth in symmetrical tiers, when established is an even more intense silvery blue	Loose, matt, bristly	Quick when established
	*Picea pungens*⁰ 'Koster' Koster's Blue Spruce	Has intensified colour in youth as well		
Blue				
	Abies procera f. *glauca* Blue Noble Fir	Specimen; foliage resembles stags-horn moss	Loose, shiny, stiffly mossy	Quick
	*Cedrus atlantica*⁰ 'Argentea' Blue Atlas Cedar	Specimen; assurgent growth, becomes layered in upcurving horizontal fronds and flat-topped with age; overlaid with exquisite silvery bloom	Loose, matt, thickly mossy	Average
	Chamaecyparis obtusa 'Crippsii' Cripps's Hinoki Cypress	Specimen; foliage to the ground	Loose, matt, plumy	Slow

nvironment

oil reference	Position	Tolerance		Ultimate spacing in metres	Notes
		Air	Soil		
loist ams, clay	Any	Dislikes over-exposure; high rainfall	Intolerant of drought; lime tolerant	8	Owing to slow early growth trees about 6 years old should be planted shallow; worth struggling with
loist ams	Any	Dislikes over-exposure	High rainfall	8	Owing to slow early growth trees about 6 years old should be planted shallow
lay	Any	Smoke tolerant; dislikes over-exposure; prefers high altitudes	Dislikes dry conditions	8	Trees should be selected for good colour and planted shallow
oams	Any	Dislikes late spring frosts; cool districts; high rainfall	Lime hating	8	Young trees transplant best; susceptible to aphid attack
loist ams, clay, nd	Open	Tolerates some smoke and salt	Lime tolerant; withstands drought	14	Specimens should be chosen for colour and planted young 1.2–1.8 m (4–6 ft) high to develop naturally
loist ams, clay	Open	High rainfall; withstands salt and smoke	Lime tolerant	8	Resents root disturbance; young pot-grown or regularly transplanted trees should be planted carefully

Alnus cordata
Italian Alder

Cryptomeria japonica
Japanese Red Cedar

Pinus heldreichii var. *leucodermis*
Bosnian Pine

Betula nigra
River Birch

Ginkgo biloba
Maidenhair Tree

Cedrus atlantica f. *glauca*
Silver Atlas Cedar

LARGE TREES

			Growth	
Dark green	*Name*	*Siting and display*	*Density, reflection, surface pattern*	*Rate*
	Abies concolor Colorado White Fir	Specimen; growth in regular tiers; rich, bold foliage	Loose, matt, ferny	Quick
	Alnus glutinosa★ Common Alder (p. 96)	Shelter, background, specimen; bold branch pattern concealed by layered foliage; beautiful catkins in spring; winter twigs purple	Loose, shiny, pitted	Average
	Chamaecyparis lawsoniana Lawson Cypress	Shelter, background, specimen; furnished with foliage to the ground	Loose, matt, ferny	Quick
	*Picea omorika*⁰ Serbian Spruce (p. 97)	Specimen; intensely narrow pagoda-like form; very symmetrical upwardly curving branches	Loose, matt, stiff mossy	Average
	Pinus jeffreyi Jeffrey's Pine	Specimen; delicate twisting branches give a snaky look	Open, matt, quilled	Quick
	Pseudotsuga menziesii Douglas Fir	Background, specimen; ragged spikes in irregular tiers	Open, matt, bristly	Quick
	Sequoia sempervirens Coast Redwood (p. 102)	Specimen; clothed to the ground with foliage, which has a deep nap	Loose, matt, feathery	Quick
	Sequoiadendron giganteum Wellingtonia or Big Tree (p. 103)	Specimen; symmetrical form clothed to ground with shaggy foliage	Loose, matt, feathery	Quick

Environment

| Soil preference | Position | Tolerance | | Ultimate spacing in metres | Notes |
		Air	Soil		
Clay	Any	Dislikes late spring frosts; cool districts; high rainfall	Lime loving	8	Young trees transplant best
Any but dry, including, swamps	Any but shade	Withstands wind, smoke and some SO_2	Drought tolerant; acid hating	14	To achieve spire shape leader must not be cut; pioneer for bleak situations, builds up fertility by fixing atmospheric nitrogen
Any	Any but shade	Withstands wind, salt and smoke; high rainfall	Lime tolerant	8	Resents root disturbance; young pot-grown or regularly transplanted trees should be planted carefully; hardy
Light, moist loams	Any	Tolerates dry conditions and smoke	Lime tolerant	5	Owing to slow early growth trees about 6 years old should be planted shallow
Dry sandy	Open	Withstands exposure		8	Resents root disturbance; young pot-grown or regularly transplanted trees should be planted carefully
Moist loams, clay	Any but shade	Frost hardy	Intolerant of lime; moisture loving but withstands drought	14	Young trees transplant best
Moist loams	Sheltered	Frost tender when young; mild districts; high rainfall		8	Young trees transplant best; full performance in south and west
Loams	Sheltered	Frost tender when young; high rainfall; mild districts		8	Young trees transplant best; full performance in south and west

LARGE TREES

Light green	Name	Siting and display	Growth	
			Density, reflection, surface pattern	Rate
	Chamaecyparis lawsoniana 'Intertexta' Gaunt Lawson Cypress	Specimen; throws out gaunt branches, which grow vertically, with dependent branchlets	Loose, matt, ferny	Quick
	Chamaecyparis lawsoniana 'Pendula Vera' Weeping Lawson Cypress	Specimen; clothed with foliage to the ground	Loose, matt, plumy	Quick
	Fraxinus excelsior★⌀ 'Pendula Wentworthii' Wentworth Ash	Specimen; upright main limbs, with foliage forming long vinelike tassels streaming gracefully down	Loose, matt, feathery	Quick
	Larix decidua European Larch *Larix × henryana* Dunkeld Larch (p. 104)	Background, specimen; pagoda-like form, feathery, airy effect; yellow-grey bark in winter; exquisite spring colour green and autumn colour bronze Is similar and vigorous	Loose, matt, bristly	Quick
	Larix laricina Tamarack	Background, specimen; delicate foliage and red bark	Loose, matt, bristly	Quick
	Metasequoia glyptostroboides Dawn Redwood (p. 105)	Specimen; autumn colour pinkish-brown	Loose, matt, feathery	Quick
	Picea orientalis Oriental Spruce 'Aurea'	Specimen; very decorative, stiff growth Has golden young shoots	Dense, matt, bristly	Average
	Ulmus angustifolia★ var. *cornubiensis* Cornish Elm	Specimen; upstanding branches barely clothed by foliage	Open, shiny, pitted	Average

Environment

| Soil preference | Position | Tolerance | | Ultimate spacing in metres | Notes |
		Air	Soil		
Any	Any but shade	High rainfall; tolerates salt and smoke	Lime tolerant	8	Resents root disturbance; young or regularly transplanted trees should be planted carefully; hardy
Any	Any but shade	High rainfall; tolerates salt and smoke	Lime tolerant	5	Resents root disturbance; young or regularly transplanted trees should be planted carefully; hardy
Loams	Any but shade	Tolerates smoke, some salt and SO_2	Lime loving	14	Gross feeder; transplants well
Loams, clay, sand	Any but shade; withstands exposure	Bleak situations; high altitudes; high rainfall		8	Young trees transplant best
Damp loams, swamps	Any but shade	Bleak situations; high rainfall		8	Young trees transplant best
Moist loams	Sheltered	Dislikes spring frosts	Slow on lime and sand	8	May require training when young
Moist loams, clay	Any	Mild districts	Tolerates lime and dry conditions	8	Owing to slow early growth trees about 6 years old should be planted shallow
Loams, clay	Any	Tolerates smoke and salt	Lime tolerant	14	Gross feeder, bad neighbour

Tsuga diversifolia
Northern Japanese Hemlock

Alnus glutinosa
Common Alder

Picea omorika
Serbian Spruce

LARGE TREES

<table>
<tr><td></td><td></td><td></td><td>Growth</td><td></td></tr>
<tr><td>Light green</td><td>Name</td><td>Siting and display</td><td>Density, reflection, surface pattern</td><td>Rate</td></tr>
<tr><td></td><td>Ulmus carpinifolia* 'Sarniensis' Jersey Elm</td><td>Specimen; elegant, upstanding branches barely clothed with foliage</td><td>Open, shiny, pitted</td><td>Average</td></tr>
<tr><td colspan="5">Yellow green</td></tr>
<tr><td></td><td>Chamaecyparis lawsoniana 'Lutea' and similar clones Golden Lawson Cypress</td><td>Sheltered background, specimen; furnished with foliage to the ground</td><td>Loose, matt, ferny</td><td>Quick</td></tr>
<tr><td></td><td>Chamaecyparis lawsoniana 'Westermannii' Westermann's Lawson Cypress</td><td>Specimen; clothed with foliage to the ground</td><td>Loose, matt, clotted</td><td>Quick</td></tr>
<tr><td></td><td>Chamaecyparis nootkatensis 'Pendula' Weeping Nootka Cypress</td><td>Specimen; narrow pagoda-like form with dependant branchlets</td><td>Loose, matt, plumy</td><td>Quick</td></tr>
<tr><td></td><td>Pseudotsuga menziesii 'Stairii' Golden Douglas Fir</td><td>Specimen; ragged spikes in irregular tiers</td><td>Open, matt, bristly</td><td>Quick</td></tr>
<tr><td></td><td>Taxodium distichum Swamp Cypress (p. 110)</td><td>Specimen; exquisite frond-like growth in layers; beautiful tender green spring colour and rich brown autumn colour</td><td>Loose, matt, fluffy</td><td>Average</td></tr>
<tr><td></td><td>Thuja plicata Western Red Cedar (p. 111)</td><td>Background, specimen; branches upwardly curving; dark yellow-green; dependent puffed growth clothes it to the ground</td><td>Loose, matt, ferny</td><td>Quick</td></tr>
</table>

Environment

Soil preference	Position	Tolerance		Ultimate spacing in metres	Notes
		Air	*Soil*		
...oams, ...ay	Any	Resists smoke and salt	Lime tolerant	14	Gross feeder and bad neighbour; closely resembling Cornish Elm
...ny	Any but shade	High rainfall	Lime tolerant	8	Resents root disturbance; young pot-grown or regularly transplanted trees should be planted carefully; hardy
...ny	Any but shade	High rainfall	Lime tolerant	8	Resents root disturbance; young pot-grown or regularly transplanted trees should be planted carefully; hardy
...oams, ...ay	Any but shade	Stands exposure	Tolerant of lime and poor dry soils	8	Resents root disturbance; young pot-grown or regularly transplanted trees should be planted carefully
...oist ...ams, clay	Any but shade	Frost hardy	Lime tolerant; moisture loving but withstands drought	14	Young trees transplant best
...et, clay	Any but shade	Prefers warm summers; smoke tolerant	Thrives in acid conditions	8	This tree likes its roots in water and thrives in swamp, although it will tolerate drier conditions
...oist ...ams	Any	Withstands wind; shade tolerant; high rainfall	Lime tolerant	8	Transplants well, useful for underfilling woodland

LARGE TREES

Grey green	Name	Siting and display	Growth — Density, reflection, surface pattern	Rate
	Chamaecyparis nootkatensis Nootka Cypress	Specimen; dull and lifeless	Loose, matt, ferny	Quick
	Larix kaempferi° Japanese Larch	Background, specimen; graceful, pagoda-like form in youth, later becoming broad spreading, with pinkish brown shoots	Loose, matt, feathery	Quick

Blue green

| | *Pseudotsuga menziesii* var. *glauca* Blue Douglas Fir | Specimen; ragged spikes in irregular tiers | Open, matt, bristly | Average |

Yellow

| | *Ulmus* 'Dicksonii' Dickson's Golden Elm | Specimen; elegant upstanding branches barely clothed with delicate foliage | Open, shiny, pitted | Slow |

Blue

| | *Chamaecyparis lawsoniana* 'Allumii' Blue Lawson Cypress | Specimen; furnished with foliage to the ground | Loose, shiny, ferny | Quick |

nvironment

oil reference	Position	Tolerance		Ultimate spacing in metres	Notes
		Air	*Soil*		
Moist loams, clay	Any but shade	Withstands wind and salt	Tolerant of poor, dry and limy soils	8	Resents root disturbance; young pot-grown or regularly transplanted trees should be planted carefully
Any	Any but shade	High altitudes, cool districts	Poor acid soils; dislikes drought and lime	8	Young trees transplant best
Moist loams, clay	Any but shade	Frost hardy	Lime tolerant; moisture loving but withstands drought	14	Young trees transplant best; these should be chosen for colour, which is variable
Loams, clay	Any but shade	Tolerates smoke and salt	Lime tolerant	8	Gross feeder and bad neighbour
Any	Any but shade	High rainfall; salt and smoke tolerant	Lime tolerant	8	Resents root disturbance; young pot-grown or regularly transplanted trees should be planted carefully; hardy

Sequoia sempervirens
Coast Redwood

Sequoiadendron giganteum
Wellingtonia or Big Tree

Larix × *henryana*
Dunkeld Larch

Metasequoia glyptostroboides
Dawn Redwood

LARGE TREES

Dark green	Name	Siting and display	Growth Density, reflection, surface pattern	Rate
	*Calocedrus decurrens*⁰ Incense Cedar (p. 112)	Specimen; growth in puffs, very formal	Dense, shiny, ferny	Slow
	Carpinus betulus★ 'Fastigiata' Columnar Hornbeam	Vertical background, specimen; graceful drooping growth; autumn colour yellow	Loose, matt, pitted	Average
	Chamaecyparis lawsoniana 'Wisselii' Wissel's Lawson Cypress	Specimen; curly spikes of crisp foliage, neat and trim	Loose, matt, mossy	Quick
	Cupressus sempervirens var. *sempervirens* Italian Cypress	Specimen	Dense, matt, spiky	Average
	Populus nigra 'Italica' Lombardy Poplar	Vertical background, specimen; shiny leaves give shimmering effect	Loose, shiny, striated	Quick
	Robinia pseudoacacia 'Pyramidalis' Columnar False Acacia	Specimen; branches somewhat tortuous; coarse, feathery, effect; white flowers in June	Loose, matt, fluffy	Quick

Light green

	Name	Siting and display	Density, reflection, surface pattern	Rate
	Betula pendula★ 'Fastigiata' Columnar Silver Birch	Specimen; a twist in the leaves on swirled branches gives dappled, liquid effect	Loose, shiny, pitted	Quick
	Chamaecyparis lawsoniana 'Erecta' Erect Lawson Cypress	Specimen; delicate, swirled angular growth, very rich foliage	Dense, slimy, ferny	Quick

nvironment

oil *reference*	*Position*	*Tolerance* Air	Soil	*Ultimate* *spacing* *in* *metres*	*Notes*
1oist *ams*	Open			5	Young trees transplant best
oams, *lay*	Any including shade	Withstands wind and smoke	Lime tolerant	5	Hardy
ny	Any but shade	High rainfall; salt tolerant	Lime tolerant	5	Resents root disturbance; young pot-grown or regularly transplanted trees should be planted carefully; hardy
oams	Sheltered	Dislikes exposure; mild districts	Lime tolerant	5	Resents root disturance; young pot-grown or regularly transplanted trees should be planted carefully; full performance only in south and west
1oist *ams, clay*	Any but shade	Not over-exposed; smoke tolerant	Lime tolerant	5	Male trees are best; inadvisable to plant near buildings; prone to disease and cv 'Plantierensis' now considered preferable
oor or *andy* *ams*	Sheltered	Smoke and salt tolerant; withstands some SO_2	Lime and somewhat acid tolerant	5	Fixes atmospheric nitrogen; useful for tips and wasteland; more suitable for street furnishing than the type; good bee tree
ands, *oams, clay*	Any but shade	Somewhat smoke, salt and SO_2 tolerant	Lime tolerant	5	A tree of medium size
ny	Any but shade	High rainfall; salt and smoke tolerant	Lime tolerant	8	Resents root disturbance; young pot-grown or regularly transplanted trees should be planted carefully; hardy

LARGE TREES

Light green	Name	Siting and display	Density, reflection, surface pattern	Rate
	Cupressocyparis leylandii Leyland Cypress (p. 113)	Specimen, neat habit; foliage to the ground	Dense, matt, ferny	Very quick
	Fagus sylvatica*⁰ 'Dawyck' Dawyck Beech (p. 114)	Vertical background, specimen; frothy fountain effect; autumn colour brown	Dense, shiny, pitted	Average
	Juniperus virginiana 'Schottii' Schott's Pencil Cedar (p. 115) 'Canaertii'	Specimen; neat compact growth Is similar	Dense, matt, mossy	Slow
	*Liriodendron tulipifera*⁰ 'Fastigiatum' Columnar Tulip Tree	Specimen; bold, handsome foliage, grey under-leaves give dappled effect; greenish-white flowers June–July; autumn colour gold	Loose, shiny, mottled	Quick
	Quercus robur* f. *fastigiata* Cypress Oak (p. 120)	Vertical background, specimen; fine striped bark; swirled growth gives effervescent, frothy effect	Loose, matt, curly	Slow

Yellow green

	Chamaecyparis lawsoniana 'Gracilis Aurea' Yellow Lawson Cypress	Specimen; clothed with foliage to the ground	Loose, matt, clotted	Quick

Grey green

	Chamaecyparis lawsoniana 'Columnaris' Columnar Lawson Cypress (p. 121)	Specimen; clothed with foliage to the ground	Loose, matt, clotted	Quick

Environment

Soil preference	Position	Tolerance Air	Soil	Ultimate spacing in metres	Notes
Moist loams, clay	Any but shade	Salt and SO_2 tolerant; high rainfall	Lime tolerant	14	Tolerates clipping
Sandy loams	Any	Dislikes over-exposure	Lime loving	8	Best planted young
Loams	Any but shade		Lime loving	5	Young trees transplant best
Loams, clay	Sun	Smoke tolerant	Acid and lime tolerant	5	Plant young in May; good bee tree
Loams, clay	Open	Withstands some SO_2 and salt	Dislikes pH extremes	8	Oaks resent root disturbance; regularly transplanted trees should be planted carefully; select for form
Any	Any but shade	High rainfall; withstands wind and salt	Lime tolerant	8	Resents root disturbance; young pot-grown or regularly transplanted trees should be planted carefully; hardy
Any	Any but shade	High rainfall; withstands wind and salt	Lime tolerant	8	Resents root disturbance; young pot-grown or regularly transplanted trees should be planted carefully; hardy

110

Taxodium distichum
Swamp Cypress

Thuja plicata
Western Red Cedar

Cupressocyparis leylandii
Leyland Cypress

Fagus sylvatica 'Dawyck'
Dawyck Beech

Juniperus virginiana 'Schottii'
Schott's Pencil Cedar

LARGE TREES

Grey green	Name	Siting and display	Growth	
			Density, reflection, surface pattern	Rate
	Pinus ponderosa Western Yellow Pine	Specimen; fine fissured fawn-brown bark; growth in pendulous fans	Loose, matt, quilled	Quick
	*Populus × canadensis*⁰ 'Eugenei' Carolina Poplar	Vertical background, specimen; silver under-leaves scintillate as they turn in the breeze	Loose, shiny, faceted	Quick
Blue green				
	Chamaecyparis lawsoniana 'Silver Queen' Silver Lawson Cypress	Specimen; clothed with foliage to the ground	Loose, dull, ferny	Quick
Blue grey				
	Juniperus virginiana 'Glauca' Silver Pencil Cedar	Specimen; neat compact growth	Loose, matt, mossy	Slow
Silver				
	Populus alba 'Pyramidalis' Bolle's Poplar	Vertical background, specimen; maple-like leaves with white reverses scintillate as they turn in the breeze	Loose, matt, mottled	Quick
Dark green				
	Zelkova carpinifolia Caucasian Elm (p. 122)	Specimen; of unique habit and delicate foliage	Loose, shiny, curly	Slow

Environment

| Soil preference | Position | Tolerance | | Ultimate spacing in metres | Notes |
		Air	Soil		
Sandy loams	Open	Withstands exposure	Somewhat drought tolerant	8	Resents root disturbance; young pot-grown or regularly transplanted trees should be planted carefully
Moist loams, clay	Any but shade	Smoke tolerant	Lime tolerant	20	Inadvisable to plant near buildings
Any	Any but shade	High rainfall; salt and smoke tolerant	Lime tolerant	8	Resents root disturbance; young pot-grown or regularly transplanted trees should be planted carefully; hardy
Loams	Any but shade		Lime loving	5	Young trees transplant best
Sands, loams, clay	Not over-exposed	Salt, smoke and SO_2 tolerant		8	Grows quickly from cuttings
Loams	Not over-exposed	Withstands some smoke	High rainfall	16	Grafted trees should be avoided

LARGE TREES

Dark green	Name	Siting and display	Growth — Density, reflection, surface pattern	Rate
	Carpinus betulus★ 'Pendula Dervaesii' Dervaes's Weeping Hornbeam	Specimen; bold and vigorous habit, branches sweeping upwards; autumn colour yellow	Loose, shiny, striated	Average
	Fagus sylvatica★ f. *pendula* Weeping Beech (p. 123)	Specimen; main limbs thrust out gauntly; from these foliage hangs in long plumes, giving very draped effect	Dense, matt, pitted	Average
	Picea smithiana West Himalayan Spruce	Specimen; graceful foliage streams from drooping branches	Loose, matt, bristly	Average
Light green				
	Fraxinus exelsior★ f. *pendula* Weeping Ash	Specimen; umbrella shaped head, all branches weeping	Loose, matt, feathery	Quick
	Larix decidua f. *pendula* Weeping European Larch	Specimen; umbrella shaped, soft, fountain effect; yellow-grey bark in winter; exquisite spring colour delicate green and autumn colour russet	Loose, matt, bristly	Quick
	Quercus robur★ f. *pendula* Weeping Oak	Specimen; growth in umbrella shaped tiers with streaming tassels; fresh effect	Loose, matt, lacy	Slow
Yellow green				
	Salix 'Chrysocoma'◊ Golden Weeping Willow (p. 126)	Specimen; beautiful yellow bark in winter; streaming plumes give graceful effect	Dense, matt, striated	Quick

Environment

Soil preference	Position	Tolerance		Ultimate spacing in metres	Notes
		Air	*Soil*		
Loams, clay	Any	Withstands wind and smoke	Lime tolerant	8	Hardy
Sandy loams	Any including semi-shade	Dislikes over-exposure	Lime loving	14	Young trees transplant best
Moist loams	Semi-shade	Frost tender in youth; high rainfall		8	Young trees transplant best
Clay	Open	Withstands wind, salt, some SO_2 and smoke	Lime loving	14	Gross feeder; transplants well
Loams, clay	Open	Bleak situations	High rainfall; high altitudes	8	Young trees transplant best
Loams, clay	Open	Stands some SO_2, salt and smoke		14	Oaks resent root disturbance; regularly transplanted trees should be planted carefully
Wet or clay	Any but shade	Withstands some salt and smoke		14	Plant large cuttings broomstick size November–March or trees less than three years old *deeper* than before

Quercus robur f. *fastigiata*
Cypress Oak

Chamaecyparis lawsoniana 'Columnaris'
Columnar Lawson Cypress

122

Fagus sylvatica f. *pendula*
Weeping Beech

LARGE TREES

Grey green	Name	Siting and display	Growth — Density, reflection, surface pattern	Rate
	Prunus × *yedoensis* f. *perpendens* Shidare Yoshino	Specimen; fragrant blush flowers March–April	Loose, matt, striated	Average
	Salix babylonica° Babylonian Willow	Specimen; streaming plumes give graceful effect, heightened in association with water	Dense, shiny, striated	Quick
	Salix × *sepulcralis* 'Salamonii' Salamon's Weeping Willow	Specimen; streaming plumes give graceful effect heightened in association with water	Dense, shiny, striated	Quick

Yellow

	Fraxinus excelsior★ 'Aurea Pendula' Weeping Golden Ash	Specimen; yellow bark in winter	Loose, shiny, feathery	Quick

Environment

Soil preference	Position	Tolerance		Ultimate spacing in metres	Notes
		Air	*Soil*		
Loams	Open	Tolerates some smoke	Lime tolerant	8	Cherries are surface rooting and should not be planted deep, consequently staking is necessary; good bee tree
Wet or clay	Any but shade	Not for cold districts		14	Plant large cuttings broomstick size November–March or trees less than three years old *deeper* than before; good bee tree; full performance in south
Wet or clay	Any but shade	For colder districts		18	Plant large cuttings broomstick size November–March or trees less than three years old *deeper* than before; good bee tree
Clay	Open	Tolerates some salt, SO₂ and smoke	Lime loving	14	Gross feeder; transplants well; a weak grower

Salix 'Chrysocoma'
Golden Weeping Willow

Crataegus crus-galli
Cockspur Thorn

SMALL TREES

Dark green	Name	Siting and display	Density, reflection, surface pattern	Rate
	Arbutus unedo★ Strawberry Tree	Specimen; many trunked; tortuous branches give rugged effect; hung with white bell flowers, and 'strawberry' fruits in autumn	Loose, shiny, striated	Slow
	Cotoneaster frigidus Himalayan Tree-cotoneaster	Specimen; prominent branch pattern, barely clothed with foliage; quantities of white flowers in spring and brilliant red fruits in autumn	Open, matt, striated	Quick
	*Crataegus crus-galli*⁰ Cockspur Thorn (p. 127)	Specimen; flat headed; tortuous horizontal branches gives layered effect; white flowers in June; autumn colour scarlet, deep red fruits persisting	Dense, shiny, curly	Slow
	Crataegus × lavallei Hybrid Cockspur Thorn	Specimen; pronounced angular branch pattern; orange-red fruits in autumn, persisting; white flowers in June; semi-evergreen	Loose, shiny, curly	Slow
	Crataegus monogyna★ Hawthorn (p. 132)	Shelter, open country; specimen; froths with fragrant white flowers in May, masses of red fruits in autumn	Dense, shiny, crinkly	Slow
	Crataegus monogyna★ 'Biflora' Glastonbury Thorn	Specimen; white, fragrant flowers in spring and during winter; red fruits in autumn	Dense, shiny, crinkly	Slow
	Crataegus oxyacantha★ May	Specimen; froths with fragrant white flowers in May; masses of red fruits in autumn	Dense, shiny, crinkly	Slow

★ Generally regarded as an indigenous species.
⁰ In author's view has excellent qualities.

Environment

Soil preference	*Position*	*Tolerance*		*Ultimate spacing in metres*	*Notes*
		Air	*Soil*		
Light loams	Open	Withstands wind and salt	Lime tolerant; mild districts	12	Best planted young in May; requires training at first; variety rubra with crimson and pink bells is handsome; good bee tree; full performance in south and west
Any well-drained	Any but deep shade	Smoke tolerant	Lime tolerant	10	Young trees require training; semi-evergreen; good bee tree
Any not water-logged	Any but deep shade	Smoke tolerant	Withstands exposure, salt and smoke	8	Resents root disturbance; regularly transplanted trees should be chosen; good bee tree
Any not water-logged	Any but deep shade	Smoke tolerant	Withstands exposure, salt and smoke	8	Resents root disturbance; regularly transplanted trees should be chosen; good bee tree
Any but dry sand	Any but deep shade	Withstands wind, smoke and salt	Lime tolerant	8	Very hardy and prickly, excellent for hedges; resents root disturbance; regularly transplanted or young trees should be chosen; good bee tree
Any but dry sand	Any but shade	Withstands wind, smoke and salt	Lime tolerant	8	Resents root disturbance; regularly transplanted trees should be chosen; good bee tree
Heavy soils	Any but shade	Withstands wind, smoke and salt	Lime tolerant	8	Resents root disturbance; regularly transplanted trees should be chosen; good bee tree

SMALL TREES			*Growth*	
Dark green	*Name*	*Siting and display*	*Density, reflection, surface pattern*	*Rate*
	*Crataegus oxyacantha** 'Punicea' Red May	Specimen; froths with scarlet flowers in May; masses of red fruits in autumn	Dense, shiny, crinkly	Slow
	*Crataegus oxyacantha* f. *rosea* Pink May	Specimen; froths with pink flowers in May; masses of red fruits in autumn	Dense, shiny, crinkly	Slow
	*Crataegus phaenopyrum* Washington Thorn	Specimen; white flowers in July; fine autumn colour and scarlet fruits, persisting	Dense, shiny, crinkly	Slow
	*Crataegus* × *prunifolia* Broad-leafed Cockspur Thorn	Specimen; umbrella-shaped head; white flowers in June, magnificent autumn colour crimson, and red fruits	Loose, matt, curly	Slow
	*Malus baccata* Siberian Crab	Specimen; froths with white flowers in April; masses of brilliant red, (cherry-like) crabs in autumn, persisting	Loose, matt, striated	Average
	*Malus coronaria* American Crab	Specimen; fragrant pinkish flowers in June; yellow-green crabs in autumn	Loose, matt, striated	Average
	*Malus hupehensis*[Ø] Hupeh Crab	Specimen; fragrant clustered apple blossoms in April; cherry-like fruits, yellow, tinged red, in autumn	Loose, matt, striated	Average
	*Malus sylvestris** Crab Apple	Open country; specimen; tortuous growth gives rugged effect; beautiful pink apple blossoms in April and clustered yellow-red crabs in autumn	Dense, matt, striated	Average
	*Malus toringoides*[Ø] Cut-leafed Crab	Specimen; growth lax and graceful; whitish flowers in May, masses of beautiful waxy fruits, yellow, flushed red in September–October	Loose, matt, striated	Average

Environment

Soil preference	Position	Tolerance Air	Soil	Ultimate spacing in metres	Notes
Heavy soils	Any but shade	Withstands wind, smoke and salt	Lime tolerant	8	Resents root disturbance; regularly transplanted trees should be chosen; good bee tree
Heavy soils	Any but shade	Withstands wind, smoke and salt	Lime tolerant	8	Resents root disturbance; regularly transplanted trees should be chosen; good bee tree
Any not water-logged	Any but deep shade	Withstands smoke, salt and wind	Lime tolerant	8	Resents root disturbance; regularly transplanted trees should be chosen; good bee tree
Any not water-logged	Any but deep shade	Withstands smoke, salt and wind	Lime tolerant	8	Resents root disturbance; regularly transplanted trees should be chosen; good bee tree
Loams, clay	Any but shade	Withstands smoke, salt and wind	Lime tolerant	8	Fruits good for jelly making; good bee tree
Loams, clay	Any but shade	Withstands smoke, salt and wind	Lime tolerant	8	Fine late-flowering species; good bee tree
Loams, clay	Any but shade	Withstands smoke, salt and wind	Lime tolerant	8	Young trees grow quickly; good bee tree
Loams, clay	Any but shade	Tolerates wind, salt and smoke	Lime tolerant	8	Young trees grow quickly; good bee tree
Loams	Any but shade	Tolerates wind, salt and smoke	Lime tolerant	8	Young trees grow quickly; good bee tree

Crataegus monogyna
Hawthorn

Morus nigra
Black Mulberry

Prunus serrula
Japanese Cherry

Amelanchier laevis
Snowy Mespil

SMALL TREES

Dark green	Name	Siting and display	Growth Density, reflection, surface pattern	Rate
	Mespilus germanica★⁰ Medlar	Specimen; crooked growth, picturesque habit; large solitary flowers in May–June	Loose, matt, striated	Slow
	Morus nigra Black Mulberry (p. 133)	Specimen; bold foliage; rugged, cumulous growth	Loose, matt, wavy	Slow
	Prunus serrula Tibetan Cherry	Specimen, for winter effect; superb shining copper bark, peeling to reveal horizontal yellow scars	Loose, matt, striated	Average
	Prunus serrulata Japanese Cherry (p. 134)	Specimen; flat-topped, marked, horizontal branch pattern; white flowers in April	Loose, matt, striated	Average
	Prunus 'Ukon' Japanese Cherry 'Ukon'	Specimen; growth drooping; pale yellow flowers in April amidst bronze foliage; autumn colour red-purple	Loose, matt, striated	Average
	Prunus 'Hokusai' Japanese Cherry 'Hokusai'	Specimen; large double pale pink flowers in April; autumn colour, salmon-orange	Loose, matt, striated	Average
	Prunus 'Tai Haku' Great White Cherry	Specimen; large white flowers, with bronze foliage in April, turning orange in autumn	Loose, matt, striated	Average

Environment

Soil preference	Position	Tolerance		Ultimate spacing in metres	Notes
		Air	*Soil*		
Loams, clay	Any but deep shade	Tolerates wind, salt and smoke	Lime tolerant	8	Very hardy; for fruits named varieties should be chosen
Warm loams	Open	Somewhat smoke tolerant	Lime and drought tolerant	10	This variety has the most palatable fruits
Loams, clay	Sheltered	Somewhat smoke tolerant	Lime tolerant	8	Cherries are shallow rooting and should not be planted deep, consequently staking is necessary; needs generous manuring for full display
Loams, clay	Sheltered	Smoke tolerant	Lime tolerant	8	Cherries are shallow rooting and should not be planted deep, consequently staking is necessary; needs generous manuring for full display
Loams, clay	Sheltered	Smoke tolerant	Lime tolerant	8	Cherries are shallow rooting and should not be planted deep, consequently staking is necessary; needs generous manuring for full display
Loams, clay	Sheltered	Smoke tolerant	Lime tolerant	8	Cherries are shallow rooting and should not be planted deep, consequently staking is necessary; needs generous manuring for full display
Loams, clay	Sheltered	Smoke tolerant	Lime tolerant	8	Cherries are shallow rooting and should not be planted deep, consequently staking is necessary; needs generous manuring for full display

SMALL TREES

Dark green	Name	Siting and display	Growth — Density, reflection, surface pattern	Rate
	Prunus 'Shimidsu' Japanese Cherry Shimidsu Zakura	Specimen; large double flowers, pink in bud turning white in May	Large, matt, striated	Average
	Prunus 'Shirotae' Japanese Cherry Mount Fuji	Specimen; growth in horizontal fans; flowers fragrant, dependent, snow-white puffy bell in April; autumn colour gold	Loose, matt, striated	Average
	Prunus 'Tao-yoma' Japanese Cherry Tao-yoma Zakura	Specimen; dense froth of luminous pink flowers amidst dark copper foliage in April	Loose, matt, striated	Slow
	Rhus typhina⁰ Stags-horn Sumach	Specimen; gaunt, spreading habit, bold foliage; crimson, 'stag-horn' fruits in autumn and superb foliage colour, orange, purple and red	Open, shiny, feathery	Slow
	Taxus baccata* 'Dovastoniana' Dovaston's Yew	Specimen; growth in assurgent, narrow fans	Loose, matt, plumy	Slow
Light green				
	Acer campestre* Hedge Maple	Specimen; neat, compact growth; autumn colour, pink-yellow	Dense, matt, mottled	Slow

Environment

Soil preference	Position	Tolerance Air	Soil	Ultimate spacing in metres	Notes
oams, ay	Sheltered	Tolerates salt	Lime tolerant	8	Cherries are shallow rooting and should not be planted deep, consequently staking is necessary; young trees may require training
oams, ay	Sheltered	Salt tolerant	Lime tolerant	8	Cherries are shallow rooting and should not be planted deep, consequently staking is necessary; young trees may require training; main trunk needs training to height of at least 1.2–1.5 m (4–5 ft)
oams, ay	Sheltered	Smoke tolerant	Lime tolerant	8	Cherries are shallow rooting and should not be planted deep, consequently staking is necessary; young trees may require training; main trunk needs training to height of at least 1.2–1.5 m (4–5 ft)
oams	Sheltered	Smoke tolerant	Lime tolerant	5	Females perform best; rich soils and manuring combined with annual pruning produce luxuriant growth with leaves 90 cm (3 ft) long
ny not ater- ogged	Any	Withstands wind and smoke	Lime loving	5	Resents root disturbance; young or regularly transplanted trees should be chosen
oams, ay	Any but deep shade	Withstands exposure, SO_2, salt and smoke	Lime tolerant	10	Makes good, high hedges; good bee tree

SMALL TREES

Light green	Name	Siting and display	Density, reflection, surface pattern	Rate
	Acer negundo Box Elder	Specimen; unusual ash-like foliage	Dense, matt, feathery	Quick
	Acer palmatum 'Osakazuki' Seven-lobed Japanese Maple	Specimen; brilliant autumn colour, fiery scarlet	Open, matt, mottled	Quick
	*Acer pennsylvanicum*⁰ 'Erythrocladum' Snake-bark Maple	Specimen; elegant branch pattern, sparsely clothed with foliage; green bark conspicuously streaked with white; winter twigs red; autumn colour yellow	Open, matt, mottled	Average
	*Amelanchier laevis*⁰ Snowy Mespil (p. 135)	Specimen; layered growth, fountain effect; powdered with creamy white flowers in April; autumn colour red-yellow	Loose, matt, lacy	Average
	Arbutus × *andrachnoides*⁰ Hybrid Strawberry Tree	Specimen; many tortuous trunks give rugged look; superb orange-brown bark peeling green; yellow flowers in March–April; orange-red fruits in autumn	Loose, shiny, curly	Slow
	Corylus jacquemontii Jacquemont's Hazel	Specimen; fine, bold foliage	Loose, matt, blobbed	Average
	Cryptomeria japonica 'Elegans' Japanese Red Cedar (juvenile form)	Specimen; many curving trunks give elegant cumulus growth of teasled woolliness; winter foliage bronzed for half the year	Dense, matt, woolly	Average
	*Magnolia kobus*⁰ var. *borealis* Northern Japanese Magnolia	Specimen; spangled with ragged white flowers in April; a veritable paper storm	Loose, shiny, curly	Average

Environment

Soil preference	*Position*	*Tolerance* Air	Soil	*Ultimate spacing in metres*	*Notes*
Moist loams	Any but shade	Withstands some smoke		12	Good bee tree
Light loams, peat	Sheltered; sun	Will not tolerate exposure; frost tender	Dislikes lime	8	Full performance in south and west
Loams, clay	Semi-shade		Lime tolerant	8	Grows quickly when young; good bee tree
Loams, clay	Open	Tolerates smoke	Lime tolerant	8	Not usually taller than 20 feet
Loams, peat	Sheltered	Frost tender; mild districts	Lime tolerant	12	Resents root disturbance; should be planted young in May; requires training at first; full performance only in south and west
Loams	Any but shade	Climatic extremes	Lime tolerant	8	Transplants well; may require training at first
Rich loams	Sheltered	Mild districts; high rainfall; withstands salt and smoke	Hates dry conditions and lime	8	Young trees transplant best; frequently not long lived; some forms are columnar
Moist loams, peat	Sheltered	High rainfall; smoke tolerant	Somewhat lime tolerant	8	Delicate root system; resents root disturance; calls for careful planting in May

142

Magnolia × *soulangiana*
Soulange-Bodin's Magnolia

Malus 'John Downie'
John Downie Crab

144

Parrotia persica
Persian Ironwood

ercis siliquastrum
ıdas Tree

SMALL TREES

Light green	Name	Siting and display	Growth Density, reflection, surface pattern	Rate
	Magnolia liliiflora 'Nigra' Purple-flowered Magnolia	Specimen; massed purple goblet flowers in April	Loose, shiny, wavy	Average
	Magnolia × soulangiana Soulange-Bodin's Magnolia (p. 142)	Specimen; massed creamy, flushed red, goblet flowers in April	Loose, shiny, wavy	Average
	'Alba Superba'	Has luminous white goblets		
	'Lennei'	Has fragrant pink, flushed red goblets in May		
	'Nigra'	Has vineous purple goblets		
	Malus floribunda Japanese Crab	Specimen; smothered with rosy-red flowers April–May and small yellow (cherry-like) fruits in autumn	Dense, shiny, pitted	Average
	Malus 'John Downie' John Downie Crab (p. 143)	Specimen; clustered white flowers in April; quantities of large conical fruits, orange and scarlet, in autumn	Loose, matt, striated	Average
	*Parrotia persica*⁰ Persian Ironwood (p. 144)	Specimen; marked horizontal branch pattern, growth in irregular layers; haze of red 'flowers' in early spring; leaves tinged copper assuming magnificent autumn colour, gold-crimson	Dense, shiny, crinkly	Slow

nvironment

Soil reference	Position	Tolerance Air	Soil	Ultimate spacing in metres	Notes
Moist loams, peat	Sheltered	High rainfall; smoke tolerant	Somewhat lime tolerant	8	Delicate root system; resents root disturbance; calls for careful planting in May
Moist loams, peat	Sheltered	High rainfall; smoke tolerant	Somewhat lime tolerant	8	Delicate root system; resents root disturbance; calls for careful planting in May
Loams, clay	Any but shade	Smoke tolerant	Lime tolerant	8	Young trees may require training; good bee tree
Loams, clay	Any but shade	Smoke tolerant	Lime tolerant	8	Young trees grow quickly; good bee tree
Loams	Any but shade	Stands wind, salt and smoke	Lime tolerant	10	Young trees require training to obtain height; very hardy

SMALL TREES			*Growth*	
Light green	*Name*	*Siting and display*	*Density, reflection, surface pattern*	*Rate*
	*Pinus halepensis*⊘ Aleppo pine	Specimen; foliage ragged and rich	Dense, shiny, spiky	Average
	*Prunus cerasus*★ 'Semperflorens' All Saints' Cherry	Specimen; white, double flowers, April and intermittently throughout summer	Open, shiny, striated	Average
	*Prunus dulcis* Almond	Specimen; deep pink flowers March–April	Open, matt, striated	Quick
	*Prunus persica* 'Magnifica' Carmine Peach	Specimen; growth spreading and lax; bright double carmine flowers in April	Loose, shiny, striated	Average
	*Prunus persica* 'Klara Mayer' Double-pink Peach	Specimen; double crimson flowers in April	Loose, shiny, striated	Average
	*Taxus baccata*★⊘ 'Horizontalis Elegantissima' Horizontal Yew	Specimen; very wide spread; yellow in spring	Dense, matt, bearded	Slow
Blue green				
	*Aralia elata* Japanese Angelica Tree	Specimen; bold, hanging, compound, leaves up to 1.2 m (4 ft) long; huge umbels of whitish flowers in August–September	Open, matt, mottled	Average

Environment

Soil preference	*Position*	*Tolerance* Air	*Tolerance* Soil	*Ultimate spacing in metres*	*Notes*
Well-drained loams, sand	Open	Resists salt; not for cold districts; frost tender when young	Fairly drought resistant lime tolerant	5	May need protection at first; resents root disturbance; young pot-grown or regularly transplanted trees should be planted carefully; can grow big in favourable conditions
Loams, clay	Any but shade	Smoke tolerant	Lime loving	8	Cherries are shallow rooting and should not be planted deep, consequently staking is necessary; good bee tree
Loams, clay	Sheltered; sun	Somewhat smoke, salt tolerant	Lime loving	8	Quickly establishes itself; good bee tree
Warm loams	Sheltered; sun	Mild districts	Lime loving	8	Full performance only in south and west; good bee tree
Warm loams	Sheltered; sun	Mild districts	Lime loving	8	Full performance only in south and west; good bee tree
Any not water-logged	Any	Withstands wind, salt, smoke	Lime loving	5	Resents root disturbance; young or regularly transplanted trees should be chosen
Poor loams	Sheltered		Lime tolerant	10	Full performance only in south

Sorbus aria
Whitebeam

Catalpa bignonioides
Indian Bean

152

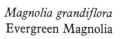

Magnolia grandiflora
Evergreen Magnolia

Prunus subhirtella
'Autumnalis'
Rose-bud Cherry

SMALL TREES

Blue green	Name	Siting and display	Growth Density, reflection, surface pattern	Rate
	Cercis siliquastrum Judas Tree (p. 145)	Specimen; rosy-purple flowers in May on bare branches; bronze 'Ash Key' fruits	Open, shiny, blobbed	Average
	Malus halliana Hall's Crab	Specimen; plum coloured bark; angular delicate branching gives effect of graceful movement; masses of bright pink bells in April; small, purple fruits in autumn	Open, matt, striated	Average
	Taxus baccata★◐ 'Glauca' Blue Jack	Specimen; growth to ground forms a spherical tree	Dense, matt, striated	Slow

Grey green				
	Crataegus laciniata Silver Thorn	Specimen; irregular somewhat gaunt, growth gives aged effect; white flowers in June; red fruits in autumn	Loose, matt, lacy	Slow
	Paulownia tomentosa◐ Foxglove Tree	Specimen; very large, broad, bold leaves; magnificent blue-purple flowers in May; full performance only in south and west	Open, matt, blobbed	Average
	Sorbus aria★◐ Whitebeam (p. 150)	Background, open country, specimen; silver under-leaves give sparkling look; masses of heavily scented, whitish flowers in May; scarlet fruits in autumn	Dense, shiny, striated	Average
	Sorbus intermedia★ Swedish Whitebeam	Shelter, background, specimen; silver reverses give a lively look to handsome oak-like foliage; masses of whitish flowers in May; red fruits in autumn	Dense, shiny, striated	Average

Environment

| Soil preference | Position | Tolerance | | Ultimate spacing in metres | Notes |
		Air	Soil		
Loams	Sheltered; sun	Dislikes exposure and spring frosts; salt tolerant	Lime tolerant	10	Full performance only in south; good bee tree
Loams	Any but shade	Smoke tolerant	Lime tolerant	8	Young trees grow quickly; good bee tree
Any but water-logged	Any	Withstands wind, smoke	Lime loving	5	Resents root disturbance; young or regularly transplanted trees should be chosen
Any not water-logged	Any but deep shade	Smoke tolerant	Lime tolerant	8	Resents root disturbance; regularly transplanted trees should be chosen; good bee tree
Loams	Warm; sheltered from spring frosts	Winter buds frost tender; smoke tolerant	Mild districts; lime tolerant	10	Useful foliage tree in districts too cold for flower performance; can grow tall; (see p. 208 for induced form)
Loams, clay and sandy	Any but shade	Withstands wind and frost, salt, SO_2 and smoke tolerant	Lime loving; drought tolerant	10	Young trees transplant best; occasionally grows to 24 m (80 ft)
Loams, clay	Any but shade	Withstands wind, salt, smoke	Lime loving; drought tolerant	10	Annual pruning makes good hedges; useful by the sea; good bee tree

SMALL TREES

Grey green	Name	Siting and display	Growth — Density, reflection, surface pattern	Rate
	Tilia oliveri Oliver's Lime	Specimen; white under-leaves give a dappled effect	Loose, shiny, mottled	Slow

Yellow green

	Name	Siting and display	Density, reflection, surface pattern	Rate
	Acer palmatum Japanese Maple (p. 160)	Specimen; growth, in tiered fans, gives Japanese effect; autumn colour, bronze	Open, matt, mottled	Slow
	Catalpa bignonioides Indian Bean (p. 151)	Specimen; bold foliage; white flowers July–August	Dense, matt, mottled	Average
	Cladrastis lutea Yellow-wood	Specimen; horizontal growth in layers; bold foliage in inverted fronds; white, fragrant flowers in June; autumn colour yellow	Loose, matt, coarsely feathery	Average
	Euonymus europaeus★ Spindle Tree	Specimen; magnificent autumn colour and flamboyant, orange, purple fruits	Loose, matt, striated	Average
	Magnolia grandiflora◊ Evergreen Magnolia (p. 152)	Specimen; fine bold foliage; superb, fragrant, white 25 cm (10 ins) 'water lily' flowers late in summer	Loose, shiny, rosetted	Slow
	Morus alba White Mulberry	Specimen; bright, bold foliage; venerable effect	Loose, shiny, wavy	Slow
	Prunus subhirtella◊ 'Autumnalis' Rose-bud Cherry (p. 153)	Specimen; very attractive shallow umbrella-shape; small leaves give airy effect; fragrant, pinkish flowers November onwards	Loose, matt, pitted	Average

Environment

| Soil preference | Position | Tolerance | | Ultimate spacing in metres | Notes |
		Air	Soil		
Moist loams	Any but shade	Somewhat smoke tolerant	Lime tolerant	12	Carefully propagated trees should be chosen
Light loams, peat	Sheltered; sun	Will not tolerate exposure; frost tender	Dislikes lime	8	Most robust Japanese Maple; full performance in south
Clay	Sheltered; sun	Smoke tolerant	Dislikes lime	12	Young trees require training; not long-lived but splendid town tree; full performance in south; can grow big; good bee tree
Clay	Sun			10	Though flowering is irregular the tree is valuable for its foliage and autumn colour
Loams	Any		Lime loving	8	Training when young makes neat, small trees
Moist loams, clay	Sheltered	Frost tender; mild districts; smoke tolerant	Lime loving	8	Resents root disturbance, should be planted in May; full performance only in south and west, elsewhere best treated as wall shrub
Warm loams	Open	Somewhat frost tender	Drought tolerant	10	Fruit, insipid
Any	Sheltered; sun	Wind, smoke and salt tolerant	Lime tolerant	8	Cherries are shallow rooting and should not be planted deep, consequently, staking is necessary

SMALL TREES

Red green	Name	Siting and display	Growth Density, reflection, surface pattern	Rate
	Malus × eleyi Eley's Purple Crab	Specimen; thickly hung with rich-red, bell-shaped blossoms in April and red-purple cherry-like fruits in autumn	Loose, matt, striated	Average
	Prunus × blireiana 'Moseri' Copper Cherry Plum	Background, specimen; bright rose flowers in March; foliage covered with fine, grey bloom	Dense, matt, striated	Average

Yellow

	Name	Siting and display		Rate
	Acer japonicum 'Aureum' Golden Downy Japanese Maple	Specimen; growth in tiered fans gives Japanese effect	Open, matt, mottled	Slow
	*Acer negundo*⁰ 'Auratum' Golden Box Elder	Specimen; suffused with golden foliage	Loose, shiny, feathery	Quick
	Catalpa bignonioides 'Aurea' Golden Indian Bean	Specimen; bold foliage; white flowers July–August	Dense, matt, mottled	Average
	Crataegus oxyacantha★ f. *aurea* Golden May	Shelter, specimen; froths with white flowers in May; masses of yellow fruits in autumn	Dense, shiny, crinkly	Slow
	Sorbus aria★ 'Chrysophylla' Golden Whitebeam	Specimen; masses of heavily scented, whitish flowers in May and scarlet fruits in autumn	Dense, shiny, striated	Slow

Red

	Name	Siting and display		Rate
	Acer palmatum 'Atropurpureum' Purple Japanese Maple 'Dissectum Atropurpureum'	Specimen; growth, in tiered fans, gives Japanese effect Has lacy foliage	Open, matt, mottled	Slow

Environment

Soil preference	Position	Tolerance		Ultimate spacing in metres	Notes
		Air	*Soil*		
Loams, clay	Any but shade	Tolerates salt and smoke	Lime tolerant	8	Young trees grow quickly
Loams	Any but shade	Somewhat smoke tolerant	Lime loving	8	Young trees grow quickly
Light loams, peat	Sheltered; sun	Will not tolerate exposure; frost tender	Dislikes lime	5	Full performance in south and west
Loams	Any but shade	Stands some smoke		12	A medium sized tree, may require pruning; good bee tree
Clay	Any but shade	Smoke tolerant	Dislikes lime	12	Young trees require training; not long-lived but splendid town tree; full performance in south; good bee tree
Loams, clay	Any but deep shade	Tolerates exposure, salt, smoke	Lime tolerant	8	Resents root disturbance; regularly transplanted or young trees should be chosen; good bee tree
Loams, clay	Any but shade	Withstands wind, frost, smoke; drought tolerant	Lime loving	10	Grafted trees grow quickest
Light loams	Sheltered; sun	Will not tolerate exposure; frost tender	Dislikes lime	8	Full performance in south

Acer palmatum
Japanese Maple

Acer platanoides 'Nanum'
Teddy Bear Norway Maple

Laurus nobilis
Sweet Bay

Salix pentandra
Bay Willow

SMALL TREES			Growth	
Red	Name	Siting and display	Density, reflection, surface pattern	Rate
	Malus$^{\emptyset}$ 'Lemoinei' Lemoine's Purple Crab	Specimen; lovely dark purple foliage; froths with masses of deep crimson flowers in April	Loose, matt, striated	Average
	Prunus cerasifera★ 'Pissardii' Purple Myrobalan Plum f. *nigra*	Background, specimen; white flowers in March; foliage covered with fine, grey bloom Has even darker colour	Dense, matt, striated	Average
Dark green				
	Acer platanoides$^{\emptyset}$ 'Nanum' Teddy Bear Norway Maple (p. 161)	Specimen; intriguing form and habit	Loose, matt, blobbed	Average
	Arbutus menziesii Madroño	Specimen; bold foliage; orange-brown bark with lovely grey bloom; erect tiers of white flowers in May; orange fruits in autumn	Open, shiny, curly	Slow
	Azara microphylla Box-leafed Azara	Specimen; delightful vanilla scented 'flowers' in February–March	Loose, shiny, lacy	Average
	Laurus nobilis Sweet Bay (p. 162)	Specimen; leaves fragrant when crushed and good for flavouring	Loose, shiny, striated	Average
	Quercus × *ludoviciana*$^{\emptyset}$ Ludwig's Oak	Specimen; beautiful coppery young growths shading to yellow, orange, red in late autumn; of glossy excellence	Loose, shiny, feathery	Average
	Salix pentandra★$^{\emptyset}$ Bay Willow (p. 163)	Specimen; pale green under-leaves give lively, dappled effect	Loose, shiny, wavy	Average

Environment

| Soil preference | Position | Tolerance | | Ultimate spacing in metres | Notes |
		Air	Soil		
Loams, clay	Any but shade	Tolerates smoke and salt	Lime tolerant	8	Young trees grow quickly
Loams, clay	Any but shade	Somewhat smoke tolerant	Lime loving	8	Young trees grow quickly; good bee tree
Any	Any but shade	Wind, smoke and salt	Lime tolerant	10	Good bee tree
Moist loams, peat	Sheltered	Frost tender; mild districts	Lime hating	12	Resents root disturbance; should be planted young in May; requires training at first; full performance in south and west
Moist loams, peats	Sheltered	Frost tender; mild districts	Lime hating	4	Full performance only in south and west
Clay	Sheltered	Smoke tolerant	Lime tolerant	5	Tolerates close pruning; useful for formalizing in tubs; full performance in south and west
Loams	Open			20	Pot-grown or regularly transplanted trees should be planted carefully
Clay	Any but shade	Tolerates exposure, high altitudes and smoke		10	Can grow large, but only shrub size at high altitudes; plant cuttings, broomstick size, or trees less than 3 years old *deeper* than before; good bee tree

SMALL TREES

Dark green	Name	Siting and display	Growth	
			Density, reflection, surface pattern	Rate
	*Taxus cuspidata*⁰ 'Contorta' Contorted Japanese Yew	Specimen; assurgent swirled growth is very fine	Dense, shiny, spiky	Slow
	Thuja orientalis f. *flagelliformis* Snaky Chinese Thuja	Specimen; growth angular and snaky	Loose, matt, scaly	Slow
Light green				
	*Acer griseum*⁰ Paper-bark Maple (p. 168)	Specimen; magnificent red-brown bark, peeling showing orange beneath; autumn colour red-orange	Loose, matt, coarsely feathery	Average
	Cordyline australis Cabbage Tree or Giant Dracaena (p. 169)	Specimen; mopheads of bold foliage and fragrant white flowers in June	Loose, shiny, plumy	Slow
	*Gleditsia aquatica*⁰ Water Locust	Specimen; graceful, airy effect; autumn colour yellow	Loose, shiny, feathery	Slow
	Populus balsamifera Balsam Poplar	Shelter, background, specimen; emanates delightful fragrance in spring	Loose, shiny, faceted	Quick
	*Rhus trichocarpa*⁰ Japanese Sumach	Specimen; enormous fan-like leaves, up to 75 cm (29 ins) long; magnificent autumn colour, orange-scarlet	Open, matt, coarsely feathery	Quick
	Sorbus aucuparia⋆⁰ Rowan (p. 170)	Open country, specimen; delicate foliage; clustered white flowers early summer and a dazzle of vermillion fruits in autumn	Loose, matt, feathery	Quick

Environment

Soil preference	Position	Tolerance		Ultimate spacing in metres	Notes
		Air	*Soil*		
Any not water-logged	Any		Lime loving	5	Resents root disturbance; young or regularly transplanted trees should be chosen
Loams	Any	Dislikes exposure; tolerates smoke	Hates lime	10	Transplants well
Loams, clay	Any but shade		Lime and fairly drought tolerant	8	Very decorative; good bee tree
Loams	Sheltered	Frost tender; mildest districts		3	Full performance only in warmest parts of south and west
Moist loams	Sun	Mild districts; smoke tolerant		8	Young trees require training; useful along watersides
Moist loams, clay	Any but shade	Stands wind and some smoke	Lime tolerant	10	Grows quickly from suckers; can grow large
Moist loams, clay	Any but shade		Lime tolerant	3	Responds to rich manuring
Sandy loams, peat	Any including semi-shade	Withstands wind, frost, smoke; high elevations and rainfall; cold districts	Acid tolerant	5	Grows quickly when young

Cordyline australis
Cabbage Tree or Giant Dracaena

Sorbus aucuparia
Rowan

Tilia mongolica
Mongolian Lime

SMALL TREES

Light green	Name	Siting and display	Growth — Density, reflection, surface pattern	Rate
	Sorbus aucuparia★ 'Edulis' Moravian Mountain Ash	Specimen; delicate, airy foliage; clustered white flowers in early summer and large, red fruits in autumn	Open, matt, feathery	Average
	Sorbus aucuparia 'Fructo Luteo' Yellow-fruited Rowan	Specimen; delicate foliage under-leaves silver; clustered white flowers early summer; yellow-orange fruits in autumn	Open, matt, feathery	Average
	Sorbus prattii Pratt's Mountain Ash	Specimen; delicate foliage; clustered white flowers in May; pearly white fruits in autumn	Open, matt, feathery	Average
	Tilia mongolica Mongolian Lime (p. 171)	Background, specimen; delicate, small leaves drooping habit; neat and compact	Dense, shiny, mottled	Average
	Trachycarpus fortunei Chusan Palm (p. 176)	Specimen; mophead of large, stiff, perfectly shaped fans gives tropical effect	Open, shiny, spiky	Slow
Blue green				
	Juniperus chinensis Chinese Juniper	Specimen; puffed growth in horizontal fans; very Chinese in effect	Loose, matt, spiky	Slow
	Salix daphnoides Violet Willow	Specimen; beautiful catkins in March; winter shoots covered with beautiful, purple waxy bloom	Loose, matt, striated	Quick

Environment

| Soil preference | Position | Tolerance | | Ultimate spacing in metres | Notes |
		Air	Soil		
Sandy loams, peat	Any but shade	Withstands wind, frost, smoke; high elevations and rainfall; cold districts	Acid tolerant; cool districts	5	Useful, edible fruit
Sandy loams, peat	Any but shade	Stands wind, frost, smoke; high elevations and rainfall; cold districts	Acid and lime tolerant	5	Useful for furnishing bleak situations and old tips
Sandy loams, peat	Any but shade		Acid and lime tolerant	5	Young trees grow quickly
Clay	Any but shade	Smoke, salt tolerant		12	Young trees have maple-like foliage; good bee tree
Rich loams	Sheltered	Dislikes exposure; not for cold districts		3	May require protection at first; benefits from rich feeding; full performance in south and west
Loams	Any but shade		Lime loving	5	Young trees transplant best
Wet or clay	Any but shade	Tolerates exposure	Lime tolerant	10	Can grow into a big tree; plant large cuttings broomstick size November–March or trees less than 3 years old, *deeper* than before; hammer in 36 cm (14 ins) lengths in populous places; good bee tree

SMALL TREES

Growth

Grey green	Name	Siting and display	Density, reflection, surface pattern	Rate
	Carpinus tschonoskii Yeddo Hornbeam	Specimen; small leaves give dripping effect	Dense, shiny, lacy	Average
	Pinus sylvestris★⊘ 'Watereri' Waterer's Scots Pine	Specimen; distinctive foliage contrasting with red-brown bark	Loose, matt, plumy	Average
	Populus tremula★⊘ Aspen	Background, specimen; scintillating leaves, constantly in movement, with liquid noise; fine catkins in February	Loose, shiny, faceted	Quick
	Sorbus discolor⊘ Chinese Scarlet Rowan	Specimen; clusters of white flowers in May; milk-white fruits and magnificent red colour in autumn	Loose, matt, feathery	Average
	Umbellularia californica Californian Laurel	Specimen; foliage scented; insignificant lemon scented flowers in April	Loose, matt, striated	Average
Yellow green				
	Catalpa fargesii Chinese Bean Tree	Specimen; white flowers in summer	Loose, matt, feathery	Average
	Gleditsia caspica Caspian Locust	Specimen; graceful, dry effect; autumn colour yellow	Loose, shiny, feathery	Slow
	Populus simonii⊘ Simon's Poplar	Specimen; lovely silver bark; prominent outwardly thrusting branches from which small leaves hang on pendulous branches; langorous effect; fragrant in spring	Loose, shiny, faceted	Quick

Environment

Soil preference	Position	Tolerance		Ultimate spacing in metres	Notes
		Air	Soil		
Loams, clay	Any but deep shade		Lime tolerant	8	Hardy
Any well-drained	Any but shade	Tolerates wind, salt, SO$_2$ and climatic extremes	Tolerates lime or acid; high rainfall	5	Pot-grown or regularly transplanted trees should be planted carefully
Any well-drained	Any but shade	Withstands cold	Tolerates lime or acid; high rainfall	8	Grows quickly from cuttings; full performance in cooler parts
Loams	Any but shade	Smoke tolerant	Acid tolerant	5	Unusual combination of decorative features
Loams	Sheltered	Frost tender; mild districts		5	Full performance only in south and west
Loams	Any but shade			5	Useful street tree
Loams	Sun	Smoke tolerant	Lime tolerant	8	Armed with formidable spines; full performance in south
Moist loams, clay	Any but shade		Lime tolerant	8	Grows quickly from cuttings

Trachycarpus fortunei
Chusan Palm

Juniperus chinensis 'Plumosa Aurea'
Chinese Golden Juniper

Ilex aquifolium
Holly

Magnolia salicifolia
Willow-leafed Magnolia

SMALL TREES

Yellow green	Name	Siting and display	Growth: Density, reflection, surface pattern	Rate
	*Juniperus chinensis*⁰ 'Plumosa Aurea' Chinese Golden Juniper (p. 177)	Specimen; puffed growth in horizontal fans; very Chinese in effect	Loose, matt, spiky	Slow
	Laurus nobilis f. *angustifolia* Narrow-leafed Sweet Bay	Specimen; leaves fragrant when crushed	Loose, matt, striated	Slow

Blue

	Name	Siting and display	Density, reflection, surface pattern	Rate
	Juniperus squamata var. *fargesii* Farges' Flaky Juniper	Specimen; red-brown bark contrasts with silvery foliage	Loose, shiny, feathery	Slow

Red green

	Name	Siting and display	Density, reflection, surface pattern	Rate
	*Populus lasiocarpa*⁰ Chinese Necklace Poplar	Specimen; grey bark, streaked black; large, bold leaves, veined red	Open, matt, faceted	Quick

Silver

	Name	Siting and display	Density, reflection, surface pattern	Rate
	Populus alba★⁰ White Poplar	Shelter, background, specimen; maple-like leaves, white reverses give dappled, scintillating effect	Loose, matt, mottled	Quick
	Pyrus salicifolia Willow-leafed Pear	Background, specimen; swirled growth gives effect of constant movement; clustered, fragrant white flowers in April	Dense, matt, striated	Average
	*Pyrus elaeagrifolia*⁰ Oleaster-leafed Pear	Similar to above but having bolder foliage	Dense, matt, striated	Average

Environment

Soil preference	*Position*	Tolerance		*Ultimate spacing in metres*	*Notes*
		Air	*Soil*		
Loams	Any but shade		Lime loving	5	Young trees transplant best
Loams	Sheltered	Frost tender; mild districts	Lime tolerant	5	Tolerates close pruning; useful for formalizing in tubs; full performance in south and west
Loams	Any but shade		Lime loving	5	Young trees transplant best
Moist loams, clay	Any but shade		Lime tolerant	12	Grows quickly from cuttings
Loams, clay	Any but shade	Withstands salt, wind, smoke	Drought tolerant	8	Grows quickly from cuttings
Loams, clay	Any but shade	Withstands salt, wind, smoke	Lime tolerant	8	Young trees require training
Loams, clay	Any but shade	Withstands salt, wind, smoke	Lime tolerant	8	Young trees require training

SMALL TREES

Growth

Yellow	Name	Siting and display	Density, reflection, surface pattern	Rate
	Populus alba⋆ 'Richardii' Richard's Poplar	Background, specimen; maple-like leaves, light under-leaves give lively dappled effect	Loose, matt, mottled	Quick
	Sorbus aucuparia⋆ 'Dirkenii' Dirken's Rowan	Background, specimen; delicate, yellow foliage, becomes yellow-green; clustered white flowers early summer and bright-red fruits in autumn	Open, matt, feathery	Average

Dark
green

	Ilex aquifolium⋆ Holly (p. 178)	Shelter, background; fragrant white flowers, May–June; scarlet berries in autumn, persisting	Dense, shiny, curly	Slow
	*Ilex × altaclerensis*⁰ 'Camelliifolia' Camellia-leafed English Holly	Specimen; brilliant large scarlet berries in autumn, persisting; the best for berry effect	Dense, shiny, striated	Slow
	Ilex aquifolium⋆ f. *bacciflava* Yellow-fruited Holly	Background, specimen; fragrant, white flowers May–June; yellow berries in autumn, persisting	Dense, shiny, curly	Slow
	Magnolia salicifolia Willow-leafed Magnolia (p. 179)	Specimen; starred with delicate, pure white flowers March–April	Loose, matt, feathery	Average

Environment

Soil preference	Position	Tolerance		Ultimate spacing in metres	Notes
		Air	*Soil*		
Loams, clay	Any but shade	Withstands wind, salt, smoke		8	Grows quickly from cuttings; useful for tips and wasteland
Loams, clay	Any but shade	Withstands wind, frost, smoke; high elevations and rainfall; cold districts	Acid and lime tolerant	5	Useful for bleak situations
Any not water-logged	Any	Withstands wind, salt, smoke	Lime and acid tolerant	8	Annual clipping makes fine, impenetrable hedges; resents root disturbance; young trees should be planted carefully in May or September; to ensure berries several trees should be planted together, or monoecious ones chosen; good bee tree
Any not water-logged	Any	Withstands wind, salt, smoke	Lime and acid tolerant	8	Resents root disturbance; young trees should be planted carefully in May or September; female; type male trees must be planted near for berries; good bee tree
Any not water-logged	Any	Withstands wind, salt, smoke	Lime and acident tolerant	8	Resents root disturbance; young trees should be planted carefully in May or September; female; type male trees must be planted near for berries; good bee tree
Clay	Sheltered	High rainfall; smoke tolerant	Somewhat lime tolerant	8	Delicate root system; resents disturbance; calls for careful planting in May

SMALL TREES

Growth

Dark green	Name	Siting and display	Density, reflection, surface pattern	Rate
	Pinus aristata Rocky Mountain Bristle-cone Pine	Specimen; neat, compact habit; growth swirled	Dense, matt, bristly	Slow
	Taxus baccata★ Yew (p. 186)	Background, specimen; growth in assurgent spikes	Dense, matt, striated	Slow
	Tsuga diversifolia Northern Japanese Hemlock (p. 95)	Specimen; growth in layered fronds, suffused with yellow in spring	Dense, shiny, plumy	Average
	Tsuga sieboldii◎ Southern Japanese Hemlock (p. 187)	Specimen; branches upwardly curving; assumes elegant, lean, typically Chinese effect	Loose, shiny, pitted	Slow

Light green

	Chamaecyparis pisifera 'Plumosa' Plumed Sawara Cypress	Specimen; fine, delicate foliage	Loose, matt, curly	Average
	Davidia involucrata◎ Handkerchief Tree (p. 188)	Specimen; conspicuous up-standing branch pattern emphasized by bold, hanging foliage, white under-leaves give dappled effect; white 'flowers' in May with scented young growths	Open, matt, mottled	Average

Environment

| Soil preference | Position | Tolerance | | Ultimate spacing in metres | Notes |
		Air	Soil		
Well-drained loams	Open			5	Resents root disturbance; young pot-grown or regularly transplanted trees should be planted carefully; tends to grow shrubby
Any not water-logged	Any	Withstands wind, smoke, salt	Lime loving	12	Resents root disturbance; young or regularly transplanted trees should be chosen; tolerates close clipping and makes good hedges but leaves may poison animals
Moist loams	Any		High rainfall	5	Might grow into a big tree under ideal conditions
Moist loams	Sheltered		High rainfall	5	Might grow into a big tree under ideal conditions
Clay	Any but shade	Stands some salt and smoke	High rainfall	8	Resents root disturbance; young pot-grown or regularly transplanted trees should be planted carefully
Clay	Open	Smoke tolerant	Lime tolerant	12	Very decorative and distinct; long to 'flower'

Taxus baccata
Yew

Tsuga sieboldii
Southern Japanese Hemlock

Davidia involucrata
Handkerchief Tree

Pinus contorta
Beach Pine

SMALL TREES

Light green	Name	Siting and display	Growth — Density, reflection, surface pattern	Rate
	Pinus armandii Armand's Pine	Specimen; delicate, loose growth	Open, matt, feathery	Quick
	*Pinus contorta*⁰ Beach Pine (p. 189)	Specimen, shelter; robust, rich foliage with fine, deep nap	Loose, matt, bristly	Average
	Prunus padus★⁰ 'Albertii' Albert's Bird Cherry	Specimen; strongly scented racemes of white flowers in May	Loose, matt, striated	Average
	Tilia × *euchlora*⁰ Caucasian Lime	Specimen; drooping branches give a swirl to neat, bright foliage	Dense, shiny, clotted	Average

Yellow green

	Name	Siting and display	Density, reflection, surface pattern	Rate
	Chamaecyparis obtusa 'Tetragona Aurea' Golden Hinoki Cypress	Specimen; neat habit; clothed with foliage to the ground	Dense, matt, plumy	Slow
	Taxus baccata★⁰ 'Semperaurea' Evergolden Yew	Specimen, background; growth in assurgent spikes, becomes flat-topped with age	Dense, shiny, striated	Slow
	Thuja standishii Japanese Thuja	Specimen; bold, handsome foliage	Loose, matt, ferny	Slow

Environment

Soil preference	*Position*	*Tolerance* Air	Soil	*Ultimate spacing in metres*	*Notes*
Well-drained loams	Open	Frost tender		8	Resents root disturbance; young pot-grown or regularly transplanted trees should be planted carefully; may grow into a large tree
Clay, poor or dry	Any but shade	Withstands wind, salt, smoke	Lime hating; withstands drought	5	Resents root disturbance; young pot-grown or regularly transplanted trees should be planted; useful pioneer for tips and wasteland
Loams	Any but shade	Cool districts, smoke tolerant	Lime loving	8	Cherries are surface rooting and should not be planted deep, consequently staking is necessary; hardy; good bee tree
Loams, clay	Any but shade	Smoke, salt tolerant	Lime loving	12	Remarkably free from noxious pests; a very desirable lime; good bee tree
Moist loams, clay	Any but shade		Lime hating; high rainfall	8	Resents root disturbance; young pot-grown or regularly transplanted trees should be chosen
Any, not water-logged	Any	Withstands wind and smoke	Lime loving	5	Resents root disturbance; young or regularly transplanted trees should be obtained; tolerates close clipping and makes good hedges but leaves may poison animals
Moist loams	Any		High rainfall	8	Transplants well

SMALL TREES

Grey green	Name	Siting and display	Density, reflection, surface pattern	Rate
	Sorbus aria★⁰ 'Majestica' Decaisne's Whitebeam	Specimen; neat habit, bold foliage; silver under-leaves give sparkling look; masses of heavily scented, whitish flowers in May and scarlet fruits in autumn	Dense, shiny, striated	Slow

Grey blue

| | *Chamaecyparis pisifera* 'Squarrosa' Fluffy Sawara Cypress | Specimen; red-brown bark and dying foliage suffuses it with warmth | Loose, matt, fluffy | Quick |

Yellow green

| | *Davidia involucrata*⁰ var. *vilmoriniana* Vilmorin's Handkerchief Tree | Specimen; conspicuous upstanding branch pattern, emphasized by bold, hanging foliage; white 'flowers' in May with scented young growth, with pink petioles | Open, matt, mottled | Average |

Yellow

| | *Ilex aquifolium*★⁰ 'Flavescens' Moonlight Holly | Specimen; fragrant white flowers May–June and scarlet berries in autumn, persisting | Dense, shiny, curly | Slow |

Red

| | *Malus* × *purpurea* Purple Crab | Specimen; wholly red; billows of cerise flowers in April; deep red crabs in autumn | Loose, matt, striated | Average |

Growth

Environment

Soil preference	Position	Tolerance		Ultimate spacing in metres	Notes
		Air	*Soil*		
Loams, clay	Any but shade	Withstands wind, frost, salt	Lime loving; drought tolerant	10	Grafted trees grow quickest
Loams, clay	Any but shade	Tolerates exposure and some salt	High rainfall	8	Resents root disturbance; young, pot-grown or regularly transplanted trees should be chosen
Clay	Open	Tolerates some smoke	Lime tolerant	12	Very decorative and distinct
Any not water-logged	Any	Withstands wind, salt and some smoke and SO_2	Lime and acid tolerant	8	Resents root disturbance; young trees should be planted carefully in May or September; female; type male trees must be planted near for berries; good bee tree
Loams, clay	Any but shade	Withstands wind, salt and some smoke and SO_2	Lime tolerant	8	Young trees grow quickly

Pinus cembra
Arolla Pine

Sciadopitys verticillata
Japanese Umbrella Pine

Thuja occidentalis
White Cedar 'Ohlendorfii'

Pinus parviflora 'Glauca'
Blue Japanese White Pine

SMALL TREES

Dark green	Name	Siting and display	Growth — Density, reflection, surface pattern	Rate
	Picea abies 'Inversa' Drooping Norway Spruce	Specimen; snaky wreathing trunk draped with clinging foliage	Dense, matt, bristly	Quick when established
	Pinus cembra Arolla Pine (p. 194)	Temporary specimen; very fine, neat habit clothed with napped foliage to the ground	Loose, matt, plumy	Average

Light green				
	Oxydendron arboreum Sorrel Tree	Specimen; very fragrant white flowers in July–August	Loose, shiny, feathery	Slow
	*Sciadopitys verticillata*⁰ Japanese Umbrella Pine (p. 195)	Specimen; tiered growth in upwardly curving fans, clothed with foliage to ground	Loose, shiny, quilled	Slow
	Thuja occidentalis White Cedar 'Ohlendorfii'⁰ (p. 196)	Shelter hedges, specimen; growth somewhat ragged Is more compact and neater	Loose, matt, ferny	Slow

Blue green				
	Chamaecyparis obtusa 'Lycopodioides' Plumed Hinoki Cypress	Specimen; neat habit; clothed with foliage to the ground	Open, matt, plumy	Slow
	Pinus flexilis Limber Pine	Specimen; symmetrical form	Loose, matt, quilled	Average

Environment

Soil preference	Position	Tolerance		Ultimate spacing in metres	Notes
		Air	Soil		
Loams, clay	Any	Dislikes open exposure	High rainfall	5	Owing to slow early growth trees about 6 years old may be planted shallow
Well-drained loams	Open		Cold districts	8	May die suddenly before reaching maturity or, rarely, grow into a big tree; resents root disturbance; young pot-grown or regularly transplanted trees should be chosen
Light or peaty loams	Open		Lime hating	8	Young trees may need training for height
Warm loams	Open		Lime hating	8	Young trees transplant best
Clay	Any	Withstands wind, salt	High rainfall; lime tolerant	8	Occasional summer pruning makes splendid hedges, useful for furnishing wet sites
Clay	Any but shade		Lime hating; high rainfall	8	Resents root disturbance; young pot-grown or regularly transplanted trees should be planted carefully; height variable
Well-drained loams	Any		High altitudes	5	Resents root disturbance; young pot-grown or regularly transplanted trees should be planted carefully; may grow big in rich soils

SMALL TREES

Blue green	Name	Siting and display	Growth — Density, reflection, surface pattern	Rate
	*Pinus parviflora*⁰ 'Glauca' Blue Japanese White Pine (p. 197)	Specimen; branches pleasantly swirled and threaded with spiky pom-poms; can spread with age	Open, matt, blobbed	Average
	Juniperus excelsa 'Perkinsii' Perkin's Greek Juniper	Specimen; graceful growth; ribbed bark	Dense, matt, plumy	Slow

Grey green

	Name	Siting and display	Density, reflection, surface pattern	Rate
	Alnus glutinosa⋆⁰ 'Imperialis' Royal Alder (p. 202)	Specimen; prominent branch pattern barely clothed with graceful foliage gives a light, airy effect	Loose, matt, feathery	Average
	Juniperus excelsa 'Stricta' Feathery Greek Juniper	Specimen; graceful growth fine brown bark	Dense, dull, feathery	Slow
	*Pinus peuce*⁰ Macedonian Pine	Specimen; fine foliage and formal shape	Dense, shiny, bristly	Average

Yellow green

	Name	Siting and display	Density, reflection, surface pattern	Rate
	*Taxodium distichum*⁰ var. *nutans* Weeping Swamp Cypress	Specimen; exquisite, pendulous, frond-like growth; beautiful, tender, green spring colour and rich-brown autumn colour	Loose, matt, fluffy	Average

Yellow

	Name	Siting and display	Density, reflection, surface pattern	Rate
	Alnus glutinosa⋆ 'Aurea' Golden Alder	Shelter, background, specimen; bold branch pattern, barely concealed with layered foliage; beautiful catkins in spring; winter twigs, purple	Loose, shiny, striated	Average to slow

Environment

| Soil preference | Position | Tolerance | | Ultimate spacing in metres | Notes |
		Air	Soil		
Well-drained loams	Open		High rainfall	5	Resents root disturbance; young pot-grown or regularly transplanted trees should be planted carefully
Loams	Any but shade		Lime loving	5	Young trees transplant best
Any, including swamps	Any but shade	Resists wind, salt smoke	High rainfall; drought, lime tolerant	10	Very hardy; best near water; young trees move best; useful pioneer for tips and wasteland
Loams	Any but shade		Lime loving	5	Young trees transplant best
Sandy loams	Any but shade		Lime tolerant	10	Young trees transplant best
Wet, clay	Any but shade	Tolerates smoke	Thrives in acid conditions	10	This tree likes its roots in water and thrives in a swamp
Any, including swamps	Any but shade	Withstands wind, salt, smoke	High rainfall; drought	10	Very hardy; best near water; useful for furnishing; young trees transplant best

Alnus glutinosa 'Imperialis
Royal Alde▸

Sequoiadendron giganteum 'Pendulum'
Weeping Wellingtonia

Taxus baccata 'Erect
Fulham Ye

Chamaecyparis lawsoniana 'Ellwoodii'
Ellwood's Lawson Cypress

SMALL TREES

Dark green	Name	Siting and display	Growth — Density, reflection, surface pattern	Rate
	*Koelreuteria paniculata*⁰ 'Fastigiata' Columnar Golden Rain Tree	Specimen; bold foliage, strong light and shade; yellow flowers July–August; autumn colour yellow	Loose, matt, coarsely feathery	Average
	Prunus 'Amanogawa' Japanese Cherry Amanogawa	Specimen; growth pleasantly swirled; clots of semi-double, white, flushed-mauve, flowers April–May	Loose, matt, striated	Average
	*Sequoiadendron giganteum*⁰ 'Pendulum' Weeping Wellingtonia (p. 203)	Specimen; only few upwardly curving side branches hang from the trunk	Open, matt, plumy	Quick
	Taxus baccata⋆⁰ 'Erecta' Fulham Yew (p. 204)	Shelter hedges, specimen; compact growth	Dense, matt, pitted	Slow

Light green	Name	Siting and display	Growth — Density, reflection, surface pattern	Rate
	Juniperus drupacea Syrian Juniper	Specimen; swirled growth gives a lively look	Loose, shiny, bristly	Slow
	Sorbus aucuparia⋆⁰ 'Fastigiata' Assurgent Rowan	Specimen; delicate foliage; clustered white flowers early summer; bright-red fruits in autumn	Open, matt, coarsely feathery	Slow
	Sorbus commixta Japanese Rowan	Specimen; clustered, white flowers in May and bright-red fruits in autumn	Loose, matt, feathery	Average

Environment

| Soil preference | Position | Tolerance | | Ultimate spacing in metres | Notes |
		Air	*Soil*		
Loams, clay	Sheltered; sun	Withstands smoke		5	Not long-lived but very handsome; good bee tree
Loams, clay	Sheltered		Lime tolerant	3	Cherries are shallow rooting and should not be planted deep, consequently, staking is necessary; good bee tree
Moist loams	Sheltered	Dislikes frost; mild districts	Dislikes lime	5	A weeping column, barely a tree, frequently distorted; young trees transplant best; tender when young; full performance in south and west
Any not water-logged	Any	Withstands wind, salt, smoke	Lime loving	5	Young trees transplant best; resents root disturbance; young or regularly transplanted trees should be chosen
Clay	Any but shade		Lime loving	5	Young trees transplant best
Loams, peat	Any but shade	Withstands wind, frost, smoke; high elevations and rainfall; cold districts	Acid and lime tolerant	5	Useful for furnishing bleak situations
Any	Any but shade	Smoke and somewhat salt tolerant	Acid, lime tolerant; cool districts	10	Not all trees display truly columnar habit, some being more spreading, though assurgent; should be chosen for shape

			Growth	
Light green	Name	Siting and display	Density, reflection, surface pattern	Rate
	Thuja orientalis 'Stricta' Pyramidal Oriental Thuja	Specimen; delicate lively foliage	Dense, matt, lacy	Slow
Blue green				
	*Chamaecyparis lawsoniana*⁰ 'Ellwoodii' Ellwood's Lawson Cypress (p. 205)	Shelter hedges, specimen; neat growth in upright fronds	Dense, matt, ferny	Slow
Grey green				
	*Chamaecyparis thyoides*⁰ 'Andelyensis' Andely's Cypress (p. 214)	Specimen; distinctive in throwing up many columnar spires, as though coppiced	Dense, matt, mossy	Slow
	Juniperus communis⋆⁰ 'Hibernica' Irish Juniper	Vertical background, specimen; neat, compact	Dense, matt, bristly	Slow
	Juniperus thurifera Spanish Juniper	Specimen; assumes picturesque lean with age	Open, matt, mossy	Slow
	*Paulownia tomentosa*⁰ (induced form) Foxglove Tree (p. 27)	Specimen; enormous leaves, 60–90 cm (2–3 ft) across, produced by pruning, provide bold foils	Open, matt, striated	Quick
	Pinus sabiniana Digger Pine	Specimen; intensely delicate, wispy growth	Loose, matt, bristly	Average

SMALL TREES

Environment

Soil preference	Position	Tolerance		Ultimate spacing in metres	Notes
		Air	Soil		
Wet or dry loams	Any	Dislikes exposure; withstands smoke	Hates dry conditions	8	Transplants well
Loams, clay	Any but shade	Withstands wind, salt, smoke	High rainfall; lime tolerant	8	Ideal for hedges, never needs clipping; resents root disturbance; young or regularly transplanted trees should be chosen
Moist loams	Open		Tolerates wet conditions	5	Pot-grown or regularly transplanted trees should be chosen
Loams	Any but shade		Lime loving	5	Young trees transplant best
Loams	Any but shade	Somewhat frost tender	Lime loving	5	Young trees transplant best
Loams	Warm, sheltered	Smoke and salt tolerant	Lime tolerant	4	Requires annual coppice pruning to produce one straight stem; suitable feeding stimulates annual growth of 3.7 m (12ft) (see p. 154 for natural form)
Well-drained loams	Open			5	Pines resent root disturbance; young pot-grown or regularly transplanted trees should be planted carefully; can grow tall

SMALL TREES

Grey green	Name	Siting and display	Growth	
			Density, reflection, surface pattern	Rate
	Pinus sylvestris★⓪ f. *fastigiata* Columnar Scots Pine	Specimen; fine orange-red and grey bark	Loose, matt, quilled	Quick
Yellow green				
	Taxus baccata★⓪ 'Fastigiata aurea' Golden Irish Yew	Specimen; obconic form; swirled growth gives graceful and lively effect	Loose, matt, striated	Slow
	Thuja occidentalis 'Lutea' 'George Peabody' White Cedar	Shelter hedges, background, specimen; neat form and habit	Dense, matt, crinkly	Slow
	Thuja orientalis 'Elegantissima' Yellow Columnar Chinese Thuja	Specimen; growth somewhat puffed	Dense, matt, plumy	Slow
Dark green				
	Crataegus monogyna★ f. *stricta* Assurgent Hawthorn (p. 216)	Specimen; prominent branch pattern; foliage crisp; white fragrant flowers in May; red fruits in autumn	Loose, matt, crinkly	Slow
	Malus prunifolia 'Fastigiata' Assurgent Pear-leafed Crab	Specimen; clustered apple blossoms in April; magnificent yellow (cherry-like) crabs hanging all along branches in autumn	Loose, matt, striated	Average
	Prunus 'Kanzan' Japanese Cherry Kanzan	Specimen; dependent, rich, double flowers April–May, amidst bronze foliage; autumn colour red-orange	Loose, matt, striated	Average

Environment

Soil preference	Position	Tolerance Air	Soil	Ultimate spacing in metres	Notes
Any well-drained	Any but shade	Wind, salt, SO$_2$ and climatic extremes	Lime or acid; high rainfall	5	Pot-grown or regularly transplanted trees should be planted carefully
Any not water-logged	Any	Withstands wind	Lime loving	4	Resents root disturbance, young or regularly transplanted trees should be chosen
Moist loams, clay	Any	Withstands wind	High rainfall; lime tolerant	8	Occasional summer pruning makes splendid hedges
Loams	Any	Dislikes exposure; tolerates salt	Hates dry conditions	8	Transplants well
Moist loams, clay	Any but deep shade	Tolerates wind, salt and some smoke	Lime tolerant	8	Resents root disturbance; regularly transplanted trees should be chosen; good bee tree
Loams	Any but shade		Lime tolerant	8	Fruits have quite good apple flavour
Loams, clay	Sheltered	Withstands smoke	Lime tolerant	10	Cherries are surface rooting and should not be planted deep, consequently, staking is necessary

SMALL TREES

			Growth	
Dark green	Name	Siting and display	Density, reflection, surface pattern	Rate
	Prunus serrulata⁰ var. spontanea Hill Cherry	Specimen; bronze leaves with white flowers in April; autumn colour red-orange to crimson; exquisitely delicate and elegant	Loose, matt, striated	Average
	Taxus baccata★ 'Fastigiata' Irish Yew (p. 216)	Specimen; obconic form; growth somewhat ropy	Dense, shiny, striated	Slow
Light green				
	Acer grosseri var. hersii Hers's Maple	Specimen; beautiful green bark streaked white; autumn colour red	Loose, matt, mottled	Quick
	Corylus chinensis Chinese Hazel	Specimen; bold, lobed foliage	Open, matt, striated	Average
	Laburnum alpinum★ Scots Laburnum Laburnum × watereri⁰ 'Vossii' Hybrid Laburnum (p. 215)	Specimen; ringlets of yellow flowers in June Specimen; improved form with 60 cm (2 ft) ringlets of larger flowers	Loose, matt, striated	Average
	Prunus persica 'Pyramidalis' Assurgent Peach	Specimen; pale pink flowers in April	Loose, shiny, striated	Average
	Stuartia sinensis⁰ Chinese Stuartia	Specimen; rich red-brown, peeling polished fawn-grey; exquisite winter effect; fragrant white flowers July–August	Open, matt, lacy	Average

Environment

Soil preference	Position	Tolerance		Ultimate spacing in metres	Notes
		Air	*Soil*		
Loams, clay	Sheltered	Withstands smoke	Lime tolerant	8	Cherries are surface rooting and should not be planted deep, consequently, staking is necessary; spreads to be flat-topped with age
Any not water-logged	Any	Withstands wind, salt, smoke	Lime loving	5	Resents root disturbance, young or regularly transplanted trees should be chosen; cv 'chestnutensis' has broader form
Moist loams, clay	Open	Smoke tolerant	Lime tolerant	8	Young trees transplant best; good bee tree
Loams	Any but shade	Climatic extremes; smoke tolerant	Lime tolerant	8	Grows large in the wild; transplants well, may require training at first
Any not water-logged	Any but shade	Smoke, salt, tolerant	Lime tolerant	8	Because of their flamboyance Laburnums should be isolated against plain backgrounds. This later flowering variety is the more useful
Warm loams	Sheltered; sun	Mild districts	Lime loving	6	Full performance in south and west; good bee tree
Warm loams	Sheltered; sun		Lime hating	8	

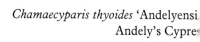

Chamaecyparis thyoides 'Andelyensi
Andely's Cypre

Laburnum × *watereri* 'Vossii'
Hybrid Laburnum

Crataegus monogyna f. *strict*
Assurgent Hawthorn

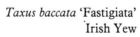

Taxus baccata 'Fastigiata'
Irish Yew

x aquifolium f. *pendula*
eeping Holly

inkgo biloba
pendula
eeping Maidenhair
ree

SMALL TREES

			Growth	
Blue green	*Name*	*Siting and display*	*Density, reflection, surface pattern*	*Rate*
	*Pinus cembroides* 'Monophylla' Single-leafed Nut Pine	Specimen; neat rhomboid form	Dense, matt, bristly	Quick
Grey green				
	*Sorbus hybrida* Bastard Service Tree	Specimen; beautiful foliage; clustered white flowers in May; bright red fruits in autumn	Loose, matt, feathery	Average
Yellow green				
	*Taxus baccata erecta*★⊘ 'Aureomarginata' Golden Erect Yew	Specimen; obconic form suffused with yellow	Loose, shiny, striated	Slow
Yellow				
	*Laburnum anagyroides* 'Aureum' Golden Laburnum	Specimen; wholly yellow; ringlets of yellow flowers in May	Loose, matt, striated	Average
Dark green				
	*Crataegus monogyna*★ f. *pendula* Weeping Hawthorn	Specimen; compact and neat; cascading white, fragrant flowers in May; red fruits in autumn	Dense, shiny, crinkly	Slow
	*Ilex aquifolium*★ f. *pendula* Weeping Holly (p. 217)	Specimen; umbrella shaped head, branches to ground, forms broad, solid mass	Dense, shiny, reeded	Slow

Environment

Soil preference	Position	Tolerance Air	Soil	Ultimate spacing in metres	Notes
Well-drained loams, clay	Open	Frost tender; salt, smoke, tolerant	Mild districts; lime tolerant	10	Resents root disturbance; young pot-grown or regularly transplanted trees should be carefully planted
Loams, clay	Any but shade	Tolerates smoke and salt	Lime tolerant	10	
Any not water-logged	Any	Withstands wind, salt, smoke	Lime loving	5	Resents root disturbance; young or regularly transplanted trees should be chosen
Any not water-logged	Any but shade	Smoke, salt tolerant	Lime tolerant	8	Because of their flamboyance laburnums should be isolated against plain backgrounds
Any not water-logged	Any but deep shade	Tolerates some salt and smoke	Lime tolerant	8	Resents root disturbance; regularly transplanted trees should be chosen; good bee tree
Any not water-logged	Open	Withstands wind, salt and some smoke	Lime and acid tolerant	8	Resents root disturbance; young trees should be planted carefully in May or September; good bee tree

SMALL TREES

Dark green	Name	Siting and display	Growth Density, reflection, surface pattern	Rate
	Prunus 'Cheal's Weeping' Cheal's Weeping Cherry	Specimen; double pink flowers in April–May	Loose, shiny, striated	Average
	Sequoiadendron giganteum[0] 'Pendulum' Weeping Wellingtonia	Specimen; only few upwardly curving side branches hang from the trunk	Open, matt, plumy	Quick
	Taxus baccata[★0] 'Gracilis Pendula' Weeping Yew	Specimen; umbrella-shaped head; branches weeping to ground	Dense, matt, striated	Slow
	Ulmus glabra[★] 'Horizontalis' Weeping Wych Elm	Specimen; arching branches and twigs; cascading, smoky effect	Loose, shiny, striated	Average
Light green				
	Betula pendula[0] 'Youngii' Young's Weeping Birch (p. 222)	Specimen; foliage hanging from gaunt limbs gives draped and very flowing effect	Loose, shiny, pitted	Quick
	Ginkgo biloba f. *pendula* Weeping Maidenhair Tree (p. 217)	Specimen; autumn colour yellow	Loose, matt, pitted	Average
	Sorbus aucuparia 'Pendula' Weeping Rowan	Specimen; cascading with clustered, white flowers in early summer and bright red fruits in autumn	Loose, matt, feathery	Average
Grey green				
	Populus tremula[★0] 'Pendula' Weeping Aspen	Specimen; faceted foliage on contorted branches gives a liquid and scintillating effect; purple catkins in February	Loose, shiny, faceted	Quick

Environment

Soil preference	*Position*	*Tolerance* Air	*Soil*	*Ultimate spacing in metres*	*Notes*
Loams, clay	Sheltered	Smoke tolerant	Lime tolerant	8	Cherries are shallow rooting and should not be planted deep, consequently staking is necessary
Moist loams	Sheltered	Dislikes frost; mild districts	Dislikes lime	5	A weeping column, barely a tree, frequently distorted; young trees transplant best; tender when young; full performance in south and west
Any not water-logged	Open	Withstands wind, salt and smoke	Lime loving	8	Resents root disturbance; young pot-grown or regularly transplanted trees should be chosen
Clay	Any but shade	Tolerates smoke, some salt and SO_2	Lime tolerant	14	Trees are grafted and may require training
Sand, well drained loams, clay	Any but shade	Smoke tolerant	Lime tolerant	8	Young trees may need training for height
Loams, clay, sand	Sheltered; sun	Smoke tolerant	Lime tolerant	8	May need training in youth
Loams, peat	Open	High elevations and rainfall; cold districts; salt, smoke tolerant	Acid tolerant	8	Useful for furnishing bleak sites
Loams, clay	Open		Lime tolerant	8	Young trees may require training

Betula pendula 'Youngii'
Young's Weeping Birch

Prunus subhirtella var. *pendula*
Weeping Spring Cherry

Cedrus atlantica 'Glauca Pendula'
Weeping Atlas Cedar

Pyrus salicifolia 'Pendula'
Weeping Willow-leafed Pear

SMALL TREES

Yellow green	Name	Siting and display	Density, reflection, surface pattern	Rate
	Morus alba 'Pendula' Weeping White Mulberry	Specimen; bright, bold foliage; venerable effect	Dense, shiny, wavy	Slow
	Prunus subhirtella var. *pendula* Weeping Spring Cherry (p. 223)	Specimen; small leaves give airy effect; rosy-pink flowers March–April	Loose, matt, lacy	Average

Silver

| | *Cedrus atlantica*⁰ 'Glauca Pendula' Weeping Atlas Cedar (p. 224) | Specimen; bold, horizontal branch pattern from which foliage streams downwards | Loose, shiny, reeded | Average |
| | *Pyrus salicifolia* 'Pendula' Weeping Willow-leafed Pear (p. 225) | Specimen; swirled growth gives effect of constant movement; clustered, fragrant, white flowers in April | Loose, matt, striated | Average |

Red

| | *Fagus sylvatica*★ 'Purpurea Pendula' Weeping Purple Beech | Specimen; main limbs thrust out gauntly, from these foliage hangs in long plumes giving very draped effect | Dense, shiny, pitted | Slow |
| | *Malus* 'Echtermayer' Weeping Purple Crab | Specimen; wholly red; cascades of clustered red flowers in April and deep red crabs in autumn | Loose, matt, striated | Average |

Environment

| Soil preference | Position | Tolerance | | Ultimate spacing in metres | Notes |
		Air	Soil		
Warm loams	Open	Smoke tolerant; somewhat frost tender	Drought tolerant	5	Young trees require training to obtain height; fruits are incipid
Loams	Sheltered; sun	Salt and smoke tolerant	Lime tolerant	5	Cherries are shallow rooting and should not be planted deep, consequently staking is necessary; young trees require training
Loams, clay	Open	Tolerates some salt and smoke	Lime tolerant; withstands drought	14	Specimens should be planted young 1.2–1.8 m (4–6 ft) high to develop naturally
Loams	Open	Smoke tolerant	Lime tolerant	5	Young trees require training for height
Loams, clay	Any including semi-shade	Dislikes over-exposure	Lime loving	10	Young trees transplant best
Loams, clay	Open	Tolerates salt, smoke	Lime tolerant	8	Young trees may require training

Bibliography

Air pollution:

Air Pollution Injury to Vegetation Raleigh, North Carolina, National Air Pollution Control Administration, US Department of Health, Education and Welfare, 1970.

Plants and Air Pollution Institute of Landscape Architects, detail sheet no. 18.

Pollution Research and the Research Councils: a report, (1971) issued jointly by the Agricultural Research Council, Medical R.C., N.E.C.R., etc. Agricultural Research Council, London.

Trees and Shrubs in Exposed Situations at University College of Wales, Penglais, Aberystwyth, 1973, BSF, Aberystwyth.

Aldous, Tony (ed.) (1979) *Trees and Buildings: complement or conflict?* RIBA and The Tree Council, London.

Anderson, A. Bertram (1965) *Gardening on Chalk and Limestone*, Collingridge, London.

Arnold-Foster, W. (1948) *Shrubs for the Milder Counties*, Country Life, London.

Bean, W. J. (1970–80) *Trees and Shrubs Hardy in the British Isles* (8th edn revised by Sir George Taylor), John Murray, London.

Bodfan Gruffydd, J. St. (1970) *Esso Refinery, Fawley: landscape report and development plan*, J. St. Bodfan Gruffydd, London.

Brimble, L. J. F. (1946) *Trees in Britain: wild, ornamental and economic, with some relatives in other lands*, Macmillan, London.

Brown, George E. (1972) *The Pruning of Trees, Shrubs and Conifers*, Faber, London.

Bush, Raymond (1947) *Frost and the Fruit Grower*, 3rd edn, Cassell, London.

Caborn, J. M. (1957) *Shelterbelts and Microclimate* (Forestry Commission bulletin no. 29), HMSO, London.

Clouston, Brian (ed.) (1977) *Landscape Design with Plants*, Heinemann, London.

Colvin, Brenda (1970) *Land and Landscape: evolution, design and control* (2nd edn), John Murray, London.

Crowe, Sylvia (1960) *The Landscape of Roads*, Architectural Press, London.

Crowe, Sylvia (1956) *Tomorrow's landscape*, Architectural Press, London.

Dallimore, W. and Jackson, A. Bruce (1966) *A Handbook of Coniferae and Ginkgoaceae*, (4th edn revised by S. G. Harrison), Edward Arnold, London.

Dictionary of Gardening, Chittenden, F. J. (ed.) (1956), 2nd edn, revised by Patrick M. Synge, OUP for the Royal Horticultural Society, Oxford, 4 vols. Supplement, by Patrick M. Synge 1969.

Edlin, H. L. (1952) *British Woodland Trees*, 2nd edn rev. 1952, Batsford, London.

Edlin, H. L. (1975) *Collins Guide to Tree Planting and Cultivation*, 3rd edn, Collins, London.

Elwes, H. J. and Henry, A. (1906–13) *The Trees of Great Britain and Ireland*, 8 vols, privately printed, 1906–13, Edinburgh.

Evelyn, John (1972) *Sylva, or a Discourse of Forest-trees and the Propagation of Timber*, facsimile edn, Scolar Press, London.

Feininger, Andreas (1968) *Trees*, Thames and Hudson, London.

Gaut, Alfred (1907) *Seaside Planting of Trees and Shrubs*, Country Life, London.

Hillier, Harold G. (1972) *Manual of Trees and Shrubs*, David & Charles, Newton Abbot.

Hoskins, W. G. (1973) *English Landscapes*, BBC, London.

Hoskins, W. G. (1977) *The Making of the English Landscape*, rev. edn, Hodder & Stoughton, London.

Howes, F. N. (1954) Bee-trees in Britain, *British Bee Journal*, 20 December.

Hussey, Christopher, (1967) *English Gardens and Landscapes 1700–1750*, Country Life, London.

Ingram, Collingwood (1948) *Ornamental Cherries*, Country Life, London.

Johnson, Hugh (1973) *The International Book of Trees*, Mitchell Beazley, London.

Kelway, Christine (1970) *Gardening on the Coast*, David & Charles, Newton Abbot.

Kelway, Christine (1962) *Seaside Gardening*, Collingridge, London.

Manley, Gordon (1952) *Climate and the British Scene*, Collins, London.

Mawson, Thomas H. (1926) *The Art and Craft of Garden Making*, 5th edn, Batsford, London.

Menninger, E. A. (1964) *Seaside Plants of the World*, Hearthside Press, New York.

Meteorological Office (1952) *Climatological Atlas of the British Isles*, HMSO, London.

Miles, Roger (1967) *Forestry in the English Landscape*, Faber, London.

Mitchell, Alan (1978) *A Field Guide to the Trees of Britain and Northern Europe*, 2nd edn, Collins, London.

Mitchell, Alan and Jobling, John (1984) *Decorative Trees for Country, Town and Garden*, HMSO, London.

Native trees of Canada (1949) 4th edn. Forestry Branch of the Department of Resources and Development, Ottawa.

Olgyay, Victor (1963) *Design with Climate: bioclimatic approach to architectural regionalism*, Princeton University Press, Princeton.

Pearce, S. A. (1965) *Flowering Shrubs and Trees*, Ebury Press, London.

Phillips, Roger (1978) *Trees in Britain, Europe and North America*, Pan Books, London.

Polunin, Oleg and Everard, Barbara (1976) *Trees and Bushes of Europe*, OUP, Oxford.

Rackham, Oliver (1976) *Trees and Woodland in the British Landscape*, Dent, London.

Rehder, Alfred (1940) *A Manual of Cultivated Trees and Shrubs Hardy in North America*, 2nd edn, Macmillan Co., New York.

Robinson, W. (1906) *The English Flower Garden and Home Grounds*, 10th edn, John Murray, London.

Specification 84: building methods and products, Part 3, Architectural Press, 1983, London.

Stamp, L. Dudley (1946) *Britain's Structure and Scenery*, Collins, London.

Stern, F. C. (1974) *A Chalk Garden*, 2nd edn, Faber, London.

Tansley, A. G. (1939) *The British Isles and their Vegetation* (rep. 1949 in 2 vols), CUP, Cambridge.

Thomas, Graham Stuart (1983) *Trees in the Landscape*, Cape, London.

Tonsley, Cecil C., (1954) Do we realise the importance of trees?, *British Bee Journal*, 3 February.

Trees for Town and Country: a selection of sixty trees suitable for general cultivation in England, 3rd rev. edn, 1961, Lund Humphries, London.

Trees in Town and City (1958), HMSO, London.

Treseder, Neil (1978) *Magnolias*, Faber, London.

Warren-Wren, S. C. (1972) *Willows*, David & Charles, Newton Abbot.

Webster, A. D. (1918) *Seaside Planting for Shelter, Ornament and Profit*, T. Fisher Unwin, London.

Wilks, J. H. (1972) *Trees of the British Isles in History and Legend*, Frederick Muller, London.

Wood, R. F. (1962) *Chalk Downland Afforestation* (Forestry Commission bulletin no. 34), HMSO, London.

Glossary

SURFACE FOLIAGE PATTERN

Description	Oxford English Dictionary definition	Author's note
Bearded	'having a beard'	Like that of a billy goat
Blobbed	'a globule . . . a small rounded mass. . . .'	Leaves appearing to hang like flattened pompoms
Bristly	'set with bristles or small stiff hairs'	As pine needles
Clotted	'run into clots'	Foliage as painted by Samuel Palmer
Crinkly	'twisted, wrinkled'	As crinkled up paper
Curly	'curling, disposed to curl'	As curly headed (not wavy or frizzy)
Faceted	'small cut faces of a diamond . . . in combination'	Breaking up a surface as if by refraction, casting light in many directions
Feathery	'resembling feathers'	A feathery texture
Ferny	'resembling fern'	As of ferns growing closely on a bank
Fluffy	'as resembling fluff; soft and downy'	Foliage looks like fluff
Frothy	'foamy'	As on a good pint of ale
Lacy	'resembling lace'	A very finely divided and delicate texture

Description	Oxford English Dictionary definition	Author's note
Mossy	'as if covered with moss'	The ferny sort of moss
Mottled	'the arrangement of a number of spots or blotches forming a mottled surface'	A ragged looking surface
Pitted	'marked or spotted with pits'	As though pricked all over with a blunt awl
Plumy	'abounding in plumes'	As ceremonial (ostrich) plumes
Quilled	'having the form of quills'	Like a porcupine
Reeded	'ornamented with reed moulding'	As of a coarse vertical thatch
Rosetted	'a bunch or knot of (leaves) concentrically disposed so as to resemble a rose'	The foliage so arranged
Scaly	'abounding in, covered with scales'	As of an alligator, coarser than a lizard, finer than a crocodile
Smoky	'having the character or appearance of smoke'	As from a smouldering bonfire
Spiky	'having the form of spikes; stiff and sharp pointed'	As though bristling with spikes
Striated	'channelled, grooved'	As though comprehensively slashed with a sharp instrument
Wavy	'full of waves'	Waves flowing into one another, not contraposed like curls
Woolly	'of the texture and appearance of wool	As a slightly fluffed up jersey

Latin name index

Italicized page numbers refer to illustrations

Common name index

Italicized page numbers refer to illustrations